UNDERSTANDING
GERALD
VIZENOR

Understanding Contemporary American Literature
Matthew J. Bruccoli, Series Editor

Volumes on

Edward Albee • Sherman Alexie • Nicholson Baker • John Barth
Donald Barthelme • The Beats • Thomas Berger
The Black Mountain Poets • Robert Bly • T. C. Boyle • Raymond Carver
Fred Chappell • Chicano Literature • Contemporary American Drama
Contemporary American Horror Fiction
Contemporary American Literary Theory
Contemporary American Science Fiction, 1926–1970
Contemporary American Science Fiction, 1970–2000
Contemporary Chicana Literature • Robert Coover • James Dickey
E. L. Doctorow • Rita Dove • John Gardner • George Garrett
John Hawkes • Joseph Heller • Lillian Hellman • Beth Henley
John Irving • Randall Jarrell • Charles Johnson • Adrienne Kennedy
William Kennedy • Jack Kerouac • Jamaica Kincaid
Tony Kushner • Ursula K. Le Guin • Denise Levertov
Bernard Malamud • Bobbie Ann Mason • Cormac McCarthy
Jill McCorkle • Carson McCullers • W. S. Merwin • Arthur Miller
Lorrie Moore • Toni Morrison's Fiction • Vladimir Nabokov
Gloria Naylor • Joyce Carol Oates • Tim O'Brien • Flannery O'Connor
Cynthia Ozick • Walker Percy • Katherine Anne Porter
Richard Powers • Reynolds Price • Annie Proulx
Thomas Pynchon • Theodore Roethke • Philip Roth
May Sarton • Hubert Selby, Jr. • Mary Lee Settle • Neil Simon
Isaac Bashevis Singer • Jane Smiley • Gary Snyder
William Stafford • Anne Tyler • Gerald Vizenor • Kurt Vonnegut
David Foster Wallace • Robert Penn Warren • James Welch
Eudora Welty • Tennessee Williams • August Wilson • Charles Wright

UNDERSTANDING
GERALD
VIZENOR

Deborah L. Madsen

The University of South Carolina Press

© 2009 University of South Carolina

Published by the University of South Carolina Press
Columbia, South Carolina 29208

www.sc.edu/uscpress

Manufactured in the United States of America

18 17 16 15 14 13 12 11 10 09   10 9 8 7 6 5 4 3 2 1

Library of Congress Cataloging-in-Publication Data

Madsen, Deborah L.
  Understanding Gerald Vizenor / Deborah L. Madsen.
    p. cm. — (Understanding contemporary American literature)
  Includes bibliographical references and index.
  ISBN 978-1-57003-856-3 (alk. paper)
  1. Vizenor, Gerald Robert, 1934– —Criticism and interpretation.
 I. Title.
  PS3572.I9Z77 2009
  818'.5409—dc22

                                              2009024338

Poems from Gerald Vizenor's books *Raising the Moon Vines,*
Matsushima, and *Cranes Arise* are reprinted with the author's
permission.

This book honors the memory of
Matthew J. Bruccoli (1931–2008).

My presence is a native trace.
My names are forever in the book.
My tease is natural reason.
My memory endures in stories.
My vision is survivance.

Gerald Vizenor

Contents

Series Editor's Preface

The volumes of *Understanding Contemporary American Literature* have been planned as guides or companions for students as well as good nonacademic readers. The editor and publisher perceive a need for these volumes because much of the influential contemporary literature makes special demands. Uninitiated readers encounter difficulty in approaching works that depart from the traditional forms and techniques of prose and poetry. Literature relies on conventions, but the conventions keep evolving; new writers form their own conventions—which in time may become familiar. Put simply, *UCAL* provides instruction in how to read certain contemporary writers—identifying and explicating their material, themes, use of language, point of view, structures, symbolism, and responses to experience.

The word *understanding* in the titles was deliberately chosen. Many willing readers lack an adequate understanding of how contemporary literature works; that is, what the author is attempting to express and the means by which it is conveyed. Although the criticism and analysis in the series have been aimed at a level of general accessibility, these introductory volumes are meant to be applied in conjunction with the works they cover. They do not provide a substitute for the works and authors they introduce, but rather prepare the reader for more profitable literary experiences.

M. J. B.

Acknowledgments

It is a great pleasure to acknowledge my enormous debt of gratitude to Gerald Vizenor, who has supported my work with characteristic humor, great generosity, and rigor. Gerald kindly sent me the manuscript of his latest novel, *Father Meme* (or *Panic Portage,* as it was then titled), and he ensured that I had a copy of the proof pages in good time to support my discussion of the novel here. Access to his curriculum vitae helped to fill in details of the many professional activities in which Gerald has been, and continues to be, involved. One of the most difficult tasks in writing a short book such as this has been finding a satisfactory way to deal with Gerald's prolific rate of publishing. While I hope I have given an overview of his achievement, limitations of space have required that I concentrate on a few key books in each of the literary genres in which he works. The problem is, of course, that each book in its way is "key." Gerald has provided valuable advice as I struggled to make these selections; he read an early draft of this manuscript and made important corrections of the facts set out here, and he twice agreed to enter into formal conversation for this book, in interviews that took place in Geneva on June 3, 2008, and in Albuquerque on October 16, 2008. He has given of his time and his thoughts in ways that I can acknowledge but never repay. This is a debt I am proud to claim.

I wish also to acknowledge colleagues who have provided an intellectual environment in which to work that is as challenging as it is fun: Simon Ortiz; Elvira Pulitano, formerly of the University of Geneva, now at California State Polytechnic University at San Luis Obispo; A. Robert Lee, who is a transnational "colleague at large" though based at Nihon University in Tokyo;

Paul Taylor, professor emeritus of the University of Geneva; Robert Warrior of the University of Illinois, who honored me and my institution with his presence; and Jace Weaver of the University of Georgia, who was instrumental to my efforts to establish an annual Native Studies Master Class in Geneva. On April Fool's Day 2004, Gerald was joined in Geneva by Helbrecht Breinig, Timothy Fox, Bob Lee, Iping Liang, Bernadette Rigal-Cellard, Paul Taylor, Yingwen Yu, and Franny Wu for a conference funded by the Swiss National Science Foundation that celebrated Gerald's literary achievements. So much of what has followed started then. I thank all the participants and especially my coorganizer Elvira Pulitano. I count myself fortunate to have had my work reviewed by such a distinguished scholar of contemporary American Literature as Jerome Klinkowitz; I thank him for his insightful comments, which have made this a much better book.

I am grateful to my graduate assistant, Erika Scheidegger, for her help with proofreading and the bibliography; Lise Magnollay, the librarian of the English Library at the University of Geneva also contributed her expertise and time in ways that have made this work possible. The University Library at the University of Cambridge offered the perfect environment in which to complete the final revisions of this book; my colleagues at Clare Hall provided a wonderfully stimulating intellectual environment, and I thank them for the Visiting Research Fellowship that brought me to Cambridge. The Department of English at the University of Geneva, the Swiss Association for North American Studies, the U.S. embassy in Bern, and the Swiss National Science Foundation have at different times contributed funding to events that brought Gerald Vizenor to Geneva, where, together with my students, I could benefit from his presence, his conversation, and his masterful, ironic humor. For this, and for Gerald's willingness to come to us as such a gracious guest, I am deeply grateful. I wish to acknowledge the generosity and hospitality of the American Studies Department at the University of New Mexico for funding my too-brief visit to Albuquerque in 2007, and I thank Laura Hall for her hospitality then and since. My husband, Mark Madsen, and our four children have embraced with warm hospitality colleagues who have, on their travels, passed through Geneva and Cambridge. I thank them for treating my friends as their own and for the generous patience with which they have lived with this project.

A staunch supporter of my work for many years was Matthew Bruccoli, founder and editor of the Understanding Contemporary American Literature series. I am proud to acknowledge my debt to him and respectfully dedicate this book to his memory.

CHAPTER 1

Overview
Gerald Vizenor in His Contexts

Gerald Vizenor is a singularly appropriate writer to appear in this series, which aims to explicate the particular difficulties posed by contemporary literature. Vizenor is a writer whose work departs radically from traditional forms and techniques, challenging existing conventions in every literary genre. Reading his work is difficult. As the Native American writer and scholar Louis Owens comments in his editorial introduction to the 1997 special issue of *Studies in American Indian Literatures* devoted to the work of Gerald Vizenor, "That he has gained world-wide critical acclaim and preeminence as the most original and critically acute of all Native American writers, while at the same time remaining virtually unknown among popular readers in America, attests to the rare nature of his achievement. . . . Vizenor's art is nearly always difficult, disturbing, disorienting, and disquieting, but it is never dishonest."[1] Vizenor himself makes a distinction between what he calls "commercial writers who are Native and literary artists who are Native."[2] It is among the latter that Vizenor counts himself, among the "original, experimental, literary artists who tell a story in a different way, and also who try to make use of Native oral experience, or any other Native experience, in an original literary way."[3]

However, Vizenor's relative anonymity among popular readers is something I want to challenge. In my view the difficulty of Vizenor's writing lies primarily in two characteristics: his original vocabulary, which is largely composed of neologisms that by their very nature must be explained to new readers, and the ironic, oppositional, or deconstructive stance he adopts in what can generally be called his "resistant" texts, that is, texts that resist easy comprehension. These two characteristics are linked: old words cannot express an original view of the world. Vizenor cannot use a language of colonial dominance and submission in order to articulate his view of social justice, he cannot deploy the mythology of European "discovery" and American "expansion" to describe the legacy of genocide that has devastated tribal communities for the past five hundred years, and he cannot articulate his vision of the future as "survivance" (his term for the resistant survival of tribal people) with a language of "victimry." So Vizenor has of necessity devised his own vocabulary to define and describe his original relation to the world. Both this vision and this vocabulary require explanation, and that is what I hope to provide in this book. Let me be clear at the outset: my concern is with helping to make his work accessible rather than providing new interpretations of individual texts. He is much read and written about in academic circles, but general readers need more encouragement to pick up and read his books. And as many people as possible need to read Gerald Vizenor. He is the most radical, even revolutionary, of contemporary Native American writers, but he is more even than this. In his critique of corporate greed and environmental devastation, of political incompetence and self-interest, and of the modern culture of simulation, celebrity, and hype, he is a radical whose ideas will provoke and challenge all contemporary readers. Vizenor's work is of concern to us all as we seek sustainable ways to move into the future.

This book is organized generically rather than chronologically to highlight Vizenor's achievements in each of the major literary genres. For reasons of space and because I give detailed readings where possible, each chapter focuses on a few key texts rather than attempting an overview of every text. With an author as prolific as Vizenor and within the constraints of the Understanding Contemporary American Literature series, it is not possible to write in detail about every publication, even though every book is certainly worthy of such attention.

Auto/Biographical Contexts

Gerald Vizenor is descended from what he calls "crossblood" or "mixedblood" origins, primarily French and Chippewa-Ojibway (Anishinaabe), and he traces his family through many generations on what is now the White Earth Reservation in northern Minnesota. He is a member of the crane clan through his father. In *Postindian Conversations* he shares with A. Robert Lee the story of his surname, which he traces to the Anishinaabe fur trader Peter Vezina, who along with all native traders was asked to choose names that were familiar to European agents.[4] Vizenor speculates that federal Indian agents mistranscribed Peter Vezina's choice of name as "Vizenor." Gerald Vizenor is among the first generation to have been born off the reservation. He was born on October 22, 1934, in Minneapolis, the son of Clement Vizenor and LaVerne Lydia Peterson. His father had moved from the White Earth Reservation to the city of Minneapolis with his mother, Alice Beaulieu, his four brothers, and two sisters. Vizenor's mother LaVerne was a third-generation Swedish American, seventeen years old at the time of his birth and a high school dropout. His parents married when his mother was three months pregnant with Gerald; they lived together for little more than a year. In 1936, when Gerald was twenty months old, his father was murdered in what remains an unsolved crime. His father's death, and the indifference of the police authorities to the crime, is a subject to which Vizenor returns repeatedly throughout his work. The infant Gerald was initially placed in the care of his paternal Anishinaabe grandmother, Alice Beaulieu. His mother made sporadic attempts to care for him, yet much of his childhood was spent in a series of foster homes and the homes of various family members. This experience was so traumatic for the child that Vizenor was rendered mute for the entire third year of his elementary schooling. But he does not recall this period of his life as wholly negative; he praises the family, teachers, and social workers who allowed him that silence rather than forcing him on to what he calls "the productive road of recitations and representations."[5] Instead he was able to develop his imaginative freedom independent of those demands of socialization, which he concedes would be the priority of social workers today. His condition was not medicalized in the sense that he was not treated for any psychological or physical handicap and, even more important, he was not made to experience his silence as something wrong and shameful. The year of silence was thus enriching for Vizenor's imaginative life, granting him an early opportunity for self-discovery and subjective exploration that nurtured his openness to nature and the physical world and to stories and myth.

Vizenor's autobiography, *Interior Landscapes: Autobiographical Myths and Metaphors* (1990), the winner of the PEN Oakland–Josephine Miles Award, provides the basis for the account of Vizenor's life that follows. However, it is worth prefacing that biography with some comments about the nature of *Interior Landscapes*. Vizenor's subtitle suggests that this book is an imaginative or fictive autobiography. In an interview with Laura Coltelli, he describes this book as self-presentation: "The facts exist in documents and in interaction, but the meaning and the value to me is of course imaginative, because it's an encounter, a double encounter. First there was the encounter of the instance, then there is the memory of the encounter which is another creative encounter, to tell the story."[6] Consequently the procedure for writing the autobiography began with the visual recollection of a sequence of scenes, which Vizenor wrote down with only one word to represent each scene. Then he selected particular scenes and made decisions about how the scenes would be presented and what details would be highlighted. Underlying this writing and editing process was another process, that of self-creation, as Vizenor explains to Coltelli: "I can't write the whole thing, nobody could and I am looking at myself in my own way: who is that, who is the self? So I imagine the self, that's where the imagination is, because I'm not a self without imagination. So I must imagine myself, whatever that self might be. I sort of told stories about the self, but in the process of telling stories about the self, I created another self, and I don't know which self you'll read out of the autobiographical stories."[7] Here Vizenor raises the issue of how to insert the autobiographical self into the narrative. He tells A. Robert Lee, "I refer to myself as a character and do so in the presence of others in the story, as my sources of memory are not separations. So to construct myself only as a first person, in that mighty, ultimate pronoun of exclusive identity, is to misplace that sense of presence and survivance."[8] Vizenor's resolution of the complex literary problem posed by including the narrative "I," but not as a separate and epistemologically superior being, is to construct the narrating "I" as a fictive autobiographical character. This strategy took some time to develop; Vizenor explains that when he was first approached to write an autobiographical essay (by Chester Anderson, who was commissioning pieces for his anthology *Growing Up in Minnesota: Ten Writers Remember Their Childhoods*), he declined the invitation "because I could not imagine writing about myself as a character. I was not an isolated self and could not think about myself without the presence of others."[9] At last he devised the technique of creating the narrating subject as one character among many. This was how he approached writing his contribution to Anderson's anthology, "I Know What You Mean, Erdupps MacChurbbs" (1976). The same technique is used in *Interior Landscapes,* and as we shall see in the chapters that follow, the problem posed by the authorial or narratorial pronoun is explored throughout Vizenor's work in poetry as well as prose.

In the autobiographical essay "Crows Written on the Poplars: Autocritical Autobiographies," in which he deliberately uses both first- and third-person personae, he writes: "Gerald Vizenor believes that autobiographies are imaginative histories; a remembrance past the barriers; wild pastimes over the pronouns."[10] Despite this claim to the fictive, a great deal of genealogical research went into the writing of *Interior Landscapes*; much of the historical detail came from archival sources such as the Anishinaabe newspaper the *Progress,* one of the first tribal newspapers, established by Vizenor's family on the White Earth Reservation in 1886 initially to oppose the Allotment Act. These details, derived from documentary sources such as the newspaper, enabled Vizenor to cross-check stories he heard from other relatives and friends. The documentary and the literary are combined also in the technical structuring of *Interior Landscapes.* A. Robert Lee suggests that the structure of *Interior Landscapes* is akin to a narrative hall of mirrors in that "there are twenty-nine sequences, each one implying at least a parallel or a mutuality with the other."[11] An example of this would be the tragic parallelism of his father's murder and the death in an industrial accident of his stepfather Elmer Petesch (who had been abandoned by LaVerne and left to care for her son) on the Christmas Eve of his fifteenth year.

Shortly after this Vizenor lied about his age and joined the Minnesota National Guard, from which he was honorably discharged a year later; when he turned eighteen he joined the U.S. Army. Following his basic training at Fort Knox in Kentucky, he was sent in the spring of 1953 to Korea, but a brief debarkation in Yokohama was prolonged and he remained stationed in Japan, first at Camp Chitose on Hokkaido Island and then at a post in Sendai.[12] At this time he developed a fascination with aspects of Japanese culture, notably the language and calligraphy, which is expressed in his substantial poetic output from the earliest haiku. In the military he worked among other things as a clerk, as a commander in the Seventieth Tank Battalion, and in the entertainment unit. When he returned to the United States, it was to Washington, D.C., where he entered the Capital Engineering Institute. During the academic year 1955–56 he studied at New York University, where his teachers of creative writing included Louise Bogan and Eda Lou Walton, before transferring to the University of Minnesota.[13] There he completed a degree in child development and Asian area studies; graduate studies in library science and Asian studies followed in 1962–64. Immediately upon graduation in 1960, he married Judith Horns, and in March 1960 his only son, Robert, was born. The marriage ended in divorce in 1969. Vizenor used his degree to obtain a post as a social worker at the Minnesota State Reformatory, a step that formally marked the beginning of a lifelong engagement in community service and activism and from which he developed a commitment to what he calls "situational ethics."[14]

Between 1964 and 1968 he was director of the American Indian Employment and Guidance Center in Minneapolis and a community organizer; he was also writing and publishing journalistic pieces concerned with the conditions encountered by Native Americans in urban environments such as Minneapolis. His reporting of two particular incidents, to which he returns in later writing, led to a full-time position as a reporter for the *Minneapolis Tribune*. He was a staff writer from 1968 to 1970, an editorial writer in 1974, and a contributing editor between 1974 and 1976. These incidents were the death in custody of Dane Michael White, a thirteen-year-old tribal boy who had run away from home and was imprisoned for a period of six weeks until he hanged himself in his cell, and the trial of Thomas James White Hawk, a mixed-blood Sioux who was sentenced to death (later commuted, in part because of Vizenor's activism) for the rape of a white woman and murder of her husband. These cases, and the issues they raise about the legal and cultural position of tribal people in urban American society, run throughout Vizenor's writing. The status of native people of mixed descent is another continuing concern and one traceable to his Anishinaabe roots. Tribal membership traditionally was based upon adoption, family, and kinship ties, not blood quantum. The idea that tribal membership belongs only to those who possess a minimum percentage of tribal blood is, in Vizenor's terms, a colonial imposition. By this he means that the federal government introduced the notion of blood quantum as part of a comprehensive program of racial classification and specifically as a way to prescribe decreasing numbers of full-blood native peoples as a solution to the "Indian problem." Vizenor is currently involved in discussions within the Minnesota Chippewa Tribe to determine constitutional reforms that would protect the tribal rights of mixed-blood family members. He is a delegate to the constitutional convention at the White Earth Reservation and is a lead writer in the effort to prepare a new constitution. "The founders, our native founders," he says, "praised the family as the foundation of a culture and new government, and that eternal humane gesture of a family, a repudiation of cold blood quantum as a measure of absence and identity, should be the essence of any new constitution."[15]

Ultimately it was to be the academic rather than journalistic world that would offer a nurturing home for the creative writing that increasingly dominated Vizenor's intellectual life. From the publication of his volumes of haiku poems—*Born in the Wind* (1960), *Two Wings the Butterfly: Haiku Poems in English* (1962), *Raising the Moon Vines: Original Haiku in English* (1964), *Slight Abrasions: A Dialogue in Haiku*, with Jerome Downes (1966), *Empty Swings: Haiku in English* (1967), and *Seventeen Chirps* (1968)—came the invitation from Lake Forest College in Illinois to teach for a year in 1970. The chair of the Department of English, George Mills, admired Vizenor's books of haiku and hired him on that basis. After a year at Lake Forest College, Vizenor returned to Minnesota to direct a teacher-training program in the Federal Desegregation Program in Minnesota's Park Rapids School District. He was then hired as director of Indian studies at Bemidji State University in Minnesota. In 1973 a Bush Foundation grant took him to study at Harvard University, and in 1976 he left the *Minneapolis Tribune*, where he had continued working as an editorial writer, and took up an academic post at the University of California at Berkeley while continuing to honor his teaching commitments at the University of Minnesota. In 1978 he was named the James J. Hill Professor at Minnesota. In 1981 he married Laura Hall, a

British student studying at Berkeley, and in 1983 they spent a year teaching as "foreign experts" at Tianjin University in the People's Republic of China. Upon their return Vizenor spent some time in Santa Fe, New Mexico, before returning to Berkeley in 1984. In 1987 he took up an appointment at the University of California, Santa Cruz, where he was provost of Kresge College during the 1989–90 academic year. In 1991 he was appointed to the David Burr Chair of Letters at the University of Oklahoma, and in 1992 he returned once again to Berkeley, this time as a tenured full professor. From 2000 to 2002 he was the Richard and Rhoda Goldman Distinguished Professor in the Division of Undergraduate and Interdisciplinary Studies at the University of California at Berkeley. He retired as professor emeritus from Berkeley in 2005 and moved to a full professorship in American studies at the University of New Mexico in Albuquerque. In 2008 he was awarded the title of Distinguished University Professor at the University of New Mexico in acknowledgment of his many career achievements.

In a recent interview Vizenor describes how of all the academic institutions in which he has worked, it is Bemidji State University that he recalls most fondly. He is most nostalgic about the years spent there as director of Indian studies, but at the same time he recalls a strong sense that he needed to learn his subject and, in order to do that, had to leave. Consequently he moved to Berkeley, where he found the intellectual challenge and stimulation he needed. The move to an endowed chair, first at the University of Minnesota and later at the University of Oklahoma, and the years as a college provost at Santa Cruz could not bring that same sense of learning the discipline. This process of learning the field of Native American or Indian studies unfolds in the sequence of Vizenor's publications that followed his move to California in 1976.[16] While he continued to write poetry, journalistic commentary on events involving native people, and editions of Anishinaabe songs and stories, he turned almost immediately to the novel, publishing *Bearheart* in 1978. In the years that followed, Vizenor produced major contributions in every genre of literature. In addition to his increasingly dominant literary voice, Vizenor developed a major presence as an agent shaping the future directions of Native American studies. From being a student of his discipline, he quickly became a decisive influence on the nature of that discipline. This central disciplinary position was achieved through great exertion and by devoting a great deal of time to traveling, talking with groups of people from all walks of life, from the academy to the community, and mentoring colleagues young and old.

Vizenor developed a professional identity as an editor of numerous important scholarly publications that influenced the way in which Native American literature is taught: the Harper-Collins anthology *Native American Literature: A Brief Introduction and Anthology* (1995) in the Literary Mosaic series under the general editorship of Ishmael Reed, the collections of scholarly essays *Narrative Chance: Postmodern Discourse on Native American Indian Literatures* (1989), and *Survivance: Narratives of Native Presence* (2008). Vizenor not only edits his own scholarly books but also mentors others through the creation of book series he oversees. For example, under his editorship the University of Oklahoma Press series American Indian Literature and Critical Studies saw the publication of more than fifty books between the creation of the series in 1990 and 2007. With Native American writer Diane Glancy, Vizenor has edited the University of Nebraska Press series Native Storiers: A Series of American Narratives, and he now edits the SUNY Press Native

Traces series. When he is not editing as either a volume or series editor, Vizenor serves on editorial boards: the American Indian Lives series at the University of Nebraska Press and, also at Nebraska, the North American Indian Prose Award. From 1992 to 1998 he served on the board of the Smithsonian Studies in Native American Literatures series; he is also a member of the Editorial Advisory Board for *ZAA* (*Zeitschrift für Anglistik und Amerikanistik: A Quarterly of Language, Literature and Culture*), published in Tübingen, Germany. He has served on the Advisory Council of the D'Arcy McNickle Center for the History of the American Indian at the Newberry Library in Chicago and has been a series advisor for *Indian America,* a documentary film series about tribal histories and cultures produced by Media Resource Associates in Washington, D.C. The great energy and commitment devoted to professional and public service evidenced by this range of involvement in Native American cultural production has shaped the academic discipline of Native American studies in decisive ways and placed Gerald Vizenor at the forefront of those who are directing the future of this scholarly field.

Vizenor also has written a substantial body of work that straddles the divide between academic and creative publications. Again these efforts shape the discipline of Native American literature in particular ways. Readers forget at their peril that Vizenor is an Anishinaabe writer first and foremost. This attention to the tribal specificity of the writer, within the generalized field of Native American or Indian studies, is an important aspect of the way in which Vizenor presents his work from a disciplinary perspective. His publications of tribal Anishinaabe stories and songs have appeared as *Escorts to White Earth: 1868–1968: 100 Year Reservation* (1968); *Anishinabe nagamon:*

Songs of the People (1970), which comprises Vizenor's interpretations of traditional Ojibway songs based on Frances Densmore's translations; and *Anishinabe adisokan: Tales of the People* (1970), a collection of tribal narratives that were originally published in the *Progress*, the White Earth Reservation newspaper edited by Theodore Hudon Beaulieu, Gerald Vizenor's great uncle. The latter two works were reprinted as *Summer in the Spring: Anishinaabe Lyric Poems and Stories* (1981). He has also published *The Everlasting Sky: New Voices from the People Named the Chippewa* (1972), *Earthdivers: Tribal Narratives on Mixed Descent* (1981), *The People Named the Chippewa: Narrative Histories* (1984), and *Touchwood: A Collection of Ojibway Prose* (1987). Also straddling the divide between academic and popular writing are the three books of journalism that have been published: *Thomas James White Hawk* (1968), *Tribal Scenes and Ceremonies* (1976; rev. ed. 1990), and *Crossbloods: Bone Courts, Bingo, and Other Reports* (1990). These journalistic pieces engage issues of pressing concern to Native American communities and individuals; they also provide illuminating points of contrast with fictive explorations of the same issues. An obvious example of this would be the call for "Bone Courts" to determine the rights of repatriation of native skeletal remains, which is first issued in an essay included in *Crossbloods* but is taken up in the drama *Ishi and the Wood Ducks* (1995), the novel *Chancers* (2000), and elsewhere in Vizenor's works. The journalism represents a form of cultural commentary, not the simple reporting of facts. The distinction among fiction, fact, documentary writing, and creative literature is further blurred by Vizenor's several published volumes of critical essays and cultural commentary, which include *Manifest Manners: Postindian Warriors of Survivance* (1994); *Fugitive Poses: Native American*

Indian Scenes of Absence and Presence (1998), which comprises the presentations originally delivered as the 1997 Abraham Lincoln Lecture Series at the University of Nebraska; *Postindian Conversations* (1999), a collection of interviews with A. Robert Lee; and *Literary Chance: Essays on Native American Survivance* (2007). These volumes of essays, in combination with his substantial body of fictional writings, have done much to underline Vizenor's reputation as the foremost Native American intellectual of our time. He cannot be encompassed by simple nouns such as "poet" or "novelist" or "scholar": he is these and very much more. The chapters that follow draw upon Vizenor's historical, journalistic, and critical writings as contexts for his creative work, which is treated according to each of the major literary genres to which he has contributed and which is outlined in what follows to conclude this account of Vizenor's career.

Vizenor turned to novel writing in the mid-1970s, after the move into academia and following his initial appointment at Berkeley. From his first novel, Vizenor has taken into the realm of fiction his concern to subvert the status quo and to mock simulations, especially the simulation that has transformed native people into "Indians." *Darkness in Saint Louis Bearheart* was published in 1978 and in a revised version as *Bearheart: The Heirship Chronicles* in 1990. His second trickster novel, *Griever: An American Monkey King in China* (1987), was inspired by the time he spent teaching in China. The trickster theme continues in *The Trickster of Liberty: Tribal Heirs to a Wild Baronage*, which followed in 1988. Relations between Europe and the Americas is the subject of *The Heirs of Columbus* (1991), which was published in time for the Columbian quincentenary, and this was followed by the novel *Dead Voices: Natural Agonies in the New World* (1992), which explores the tension between tribal storytelling and European "wordies," who are imprisoned in language and seek to imprison the world in static names. *Hotline Healers: An Almost Browne Novel* (1997) resumes the comic trickster theme; in the novels that follow, however, the trickster narrative becomes much darker and more sober as Vizenor turns to urgent social issues: the repatriation of native skeletal remains in *Chancers* (2000), the aftermath of the nuclear bombing of Japan in *Hiroshima Bugi: Atomu 57* (2003), and child sexual abuse by reservation priests in *Father Meme* (2008). Vizenor's short stories, some of which are later incorporated into his longer narratives, have appeared in major newspapers, magazines, and literary journals; collections of these include *Wordarrows: Indians and Whites in the New Fur Trade* (1978) and *Landfill Meditation: Crossblood Stories* (1991). In 1983 Vizenor extended his trickster narratives from the genre of fiction to that of the screenplay. *Harold of Orange* was produced as a film and screened at the Sundance Festival in Utah; this foray into dramatic writing was followed, after a period of more than a decade, by the play *Ishi and the Wood Ducks* (1995). As well as the early volumes of Vizenor's haiku poetry listed above, *Seventeen Chirps* appeared in 1968, followed by *Matsushima: Pine Islands* (1984), *Water Striders* (1989), and *Cranes Arise* (1999). The volume of lyrical poems *Almost Ashore* was published in 2006, and in the same year Vizenor continued his exploration of somber themes with the publication of his first epic poem, *Bear Island: The War at Sugar Point*, a historical account of the last of the "Indian Wars."

Vizenor's eminence in the field of Native American literature is sustained not only by his prolific rate of publication but also by an extensive program of speaking engagements both in the United States and abroad. He has lectured across the United

States: extensively in California and Minnesota but also at events from Las Vegas to Chicago; from Milwaukee to Olympia, Washington; from Portland Oregon, to Norman, Oklahoma; and from Fairbanks and Anchorage in Alaska to Albany, New York. In 1991, to take a randomly selected year, he gave thirteen presentations in very diverse contexts, such as the United States Information Agency–sponsored lecture tour Native American Indians in Literature and Film at universities in more than a dozen cities in Germany, Italy, and Switzerland; the conference on Native Americans and public education organized by the Confederated Tribes of the Warm Springs Reservation in Oregon, where he gave the keynote lecture, "Burdens of Failure in Education"; and the seminar and workshop with public school teachers hosted by the Evergreen College in Olympia, Washington. Internationally he has lectured across Canada: in Vancouver, Edmonton, Montreal, and at the First Nations House of Learning, the Saskatchewan Indian Federated College, the University of Regina, and the University of Alberta. International demand for his lectures has taken him to Germany, Italy, Switzerland, France, the Netherlands, Spain, Austria, England, and Georgetown, Guyana. His lecture tours have also included stops in Japan, where he has presented his work in Tokyo, Fukuoka, Kobe, Hiroshima, Kyoto, Nagoya, Osaka, and Sendai. His work has been translated into many languages, including Japanese, French, Italian, Russian, and German.

Vizenor's eminence in the discipline of Native American literature and his position as one of America's foremost contemporary creative writers has been recognized with multiple awards: the 2005 Distinguished Achievement Award of the Western Literature Association, the 2005 Distinguished Minnesotan Award, and a Lifetime Literary Achievement Award from the Native

Writer's Circle of the Americas in 2001. His professional achievement in literature was recognized by the California Arts Council in 1989 with an Artists Fellowship in Literature. He has twice been recipient of the PEN Oakland–Josephine Miles Award for Excellence in Literature: in 1996 for his anthology *Native American Literature* and in 1990 for *Interior Landscapes: Autobiographical Myths and Metaphors.* His novel *Griever: An American Monkey King in China* was awarded a 1988 American Book Award and a 1986 New York Fiction Collective Award. Evidence of Vizenor's public popularity is also bountiful. In 2000 he was appointed Literary Laureate by the San Francisco Public Library, he was named one of "100 Visionaries" by the editors of the *Utne Reader* in 1995, and he was awarded the honorary degree of Doctor of Humane Letters by Macalester College in Saint Paul, Minnesota, in May 1999.

Scholars who wish to consult the manuscript archives of Vizenor's work are directed to two collections. The American Literature Manuscripts Collection of the Beinecke Library at Yale University acquired manuscripts, letters, and other literary material in 2000, 2004, and 2008. In 2000 the Minnesota Historical Society established a database biography and manuscript collection devoted to Gerald Vizenor as part of the Minnesota Author Biographies Project.

Vizenor's literary output is prodigious and shows no sign of abating as he reaches the middle years of his seventh decade. In the course of a writing career that spans nearly half a century, Gerald Vizenor has contributed to and extended the possibilities of every literary genre: the novel, short fiction, poetry, drama (including the modern genre of the screenplay), journalism, autobiography, history, and social commentary. He is more than a writer: Gerald Vizenor is a highly influential intellectual who has redefined the field of Native American studies through his mentoring of young writers and academics as well as through his own work. In particular his efforts to deconstruct the notion of "the Indian" as a colonial imposition that bears no relation to the tribal identities of real native people has proved controversial, though productively so, inaugurating an important conversation about what the concept of "Indians" means and how the culture of American "Indians" should be studied. He describes himself as both an American Indian writer and a writer who just happens to be a Native American Indian—"a contradiction. I believe my particular presentation of the mythic experience and the energy I go after, and the imagery in poetry, I celebrate from tribal sources. It's universal, too, but I celebrate from tribal sources. So that makes me an Indian poet. But I write poetry which doesn't look like that." He concludes with characteristic irony, "I think most Indian poets now prefer to write their poetry and not announce their obligation to invented categories."[17]

Native Contexts

The field of American Indian or Native American literature is often identified with the historical moment known as the Native American Renaissance. This cultural phenomenon was so named by the critic Kenneth Lincoln in his 1983 book, *Native American Renaissance*.[18] This "rebirth" of Native American literature, according to Lincoln, was marked by the watershed event of the awarding of the 1968 Pulitzer Prize to Kiowa writer N. Scott Momaday for his novel *House Made of Dawn*. This award coincided with the historical emergence of a group of Native Americans who were the first to achieve national and international popular recognition. These writers include Leslie Marmon Silko, James Welch, Simon Ortiz, Paula Gunn Allen,

Joy Harjo, Louise Erdrich, and Gerald Vizenor. This new profile for Native American literature and a growing readership were enabled, in part, by the creation of disciplinary infrastructure that helped promote the study of Native American literature: university departments devoted to Native American studies and the participation of writers such as Vizenor in these disciplinary endeavors, the establishment of scholarly journals such as *Studies in American Indian Literatures* and, more recently, the creation of a professional association for Native American and indigenous studies. However, the concept of a historical break, occurring in 1968, that separates two distinct periods within the Native American literary tradition has been widely criticized, not least by Vizenor himself, for obstructing an appreciation of the continuities that mark Native American literature and for obscuring the achievements of earlier writers such as William Apess, John Rollin Ridge, and John Joseph Mathews. Additionally the privilege accorded to written texts produced in English as part of this "renaissance," as opposed to oral works created in tribal languages, has been criticized.

Vizenor consistently identifies his work with the tribal, oral tradition, and he describes his style of writing as a visual experience: "It doesn't come as a text, it's an event."[19] In this way Vizenor identifies his work as that of an Anishinaabe writer. In *The Everlasting Sky* (1972) he observes that the "*oshki anishinabe* writer is a visual thinker soaring on the rhythms of the woodland past through the gestures of the present."[20] The story or poem follows from a scene that is visualized, recalled, or imagined. This then affects the literary style of his writing. Stories begin not with the concept of motivation but with the scene out of which the story will arise: "There isn't any motivation, it's just the action, the motion, that's how a trickster story might begin," Vizenor explains to Laura Coltelli. "Things just happen, you cannot account for them, although you are responsible for them because of things you've done or haven't done."[21] Motivation is linear and thus reduces the opportunities for chance events and encounters in the narrative, while action is more unpredictable and less constrained by causal linkages. Underlining the importance of oral storytelling in his writing, especially his novels and stories, Vizenor often creates scenes in which characters listen or read, or in which characters listen to or read each other's stories. In this way Vizenor constructs within his texts a fictive readership and thus confronts the primary difference between oral and written stories: the absence of community, which, in written texts, is replaced by the individual reader. Given the very different situation of literary reception, when an individual reader opens a book, Vizenor explains to John Purdy and Blake Hausman, "you have to create a play of readers and listeners in the story itself."[22]

The historical nature of the tribal oral tradition presents a particular difficulty for any contemporary native writer who is aware of the irretrievable quality of the past. Robert Silberman notes the difficulty presented by "the opposition between the fading or even lost world of unself-conscious tribal myth in an oral tradition and the world of print . . . in which the values of the earlier tradition can be preserved but must be transformed in order to do so. The situation demands great self-consciousness and irony."[23] Irony is one of several techniques that Vizenor uses to access particular aspects of the oral tradition without denying his own position, which is clearly located in modernity. One of the characteristics of the oral tradition that marks Vizenor's work is the use of the same characters, settings, and ideas repetitively in story after story, poem after poem. There is no fixed "scriptural" version of any Vizenor text; all are available for revision and reinterpretation. Alan Velie remarks of this quality in Vizenor's writing: "One of the appealing things about Vizenor's works is that they appear to be one huge moebius strip. Never mind that there are poems, essays, stories, and novels. They seem to be parts of a unified whole because the same characters scuttle in and out, often telling the same stories."[24] Velie made this comment in his 1982 book, *Four American Indian Literary Masters*, and the truth of his observation has been consolidated by Vizenor's published work in the period since then.

The repetition of characters, images, and ideas across a range of texts lends these literary devices a reality that is independent of any specific text. The reader is placed in a position of recalling a character or a turn of phrase from an earlier story or poem; the visual memory that inspires Vizenor's writing of the text also inspires the reader's interpretation of it. As Vizenor explains, "My purpose is lyrical, to remind the reader of a metaphysical lyric value and sometimes I will repeat the same sentence or phrase as a kind of lyrical visual device."[25] The language that Vizenor uses to describe his aesthetic clearly derives from his writing of poetry and particularly the discipline of composing haiku poems. He describes his approach to writing as a transformative process: "What I do is something I learned in haiku, which is a contradiction, but I start with an initial natural metaphor and through that you can immediately engage the reader in a time, a place, a sense, certainly the season, even if it doesn't establish motivation. So I build on those metaphors of time, place, season usually in opening a chapter."[26] When asked, in a 1981 interview, how he goes about the process of writing, Vizenor replied, "I can think of three ways I write: by inspiration, by torturous attention, and by schedule. The most pleasant, of course, is inspiration. The most productive is the forced, tor-turous way. The schedule kind doesn't necessarily work for me. I set up a time and work into it awkwardly. I often avoid sched-ules. In the rest of my life, I fight schedules. But I become very compulsive when I set out to do something. If it is a book, a whole book, I try to find the time to do it, and I surround my whole life with it."[27]

Asked to characterize Native American literature (in contrast with nonnative writings), Vizenor tells Hartwig Isernhagen that "the authors make active and immediate use of mythic material that's associated with traditional experience"; of his own writing he notes that the use of myth and published tribal documentary sources is, along with the oral tradition, the most important dis-tinguishing feature of native writing.[28] Elsewhere in the same interview, Vizenor notes his good fortune as an Anishinaabe writer to have inherited a long history of tribal writing about tribal experience; even if he cannot share the values expressed by early Anishinaabeg writers such as George Copway, he neverthe-less has the advantage that Copway's vision and experience have been preserved in writing.[29]

Post/Modern Contexts

It can be productive to ask of Vizenor's work not whether he is a postmodernist writer, as some critics suggest, but why the con-cept of postmodernism should be invoked in relation to his writ-ing. The answer lies in the double nature of Vizenor's approach to writing as a tribal author. On the one hand, he seeks to articu-late a vision that is grounded in his tribal experience; on the other hand, he is aware that this tribal context has been misap-propriated by the dominant culture within a paradigm of sav-agery versus civilization—those "wicked terms," as he refers to them in *The Everlasting Sky: New Voices from the People Named the Chippewa* (1972). The ironic subtitle of this book captures Vizenor's point that the "Chippewa" have been subjected to a colonialist act of naming. They call themselves Anishinaabeg but have been named Chippewa by European colonists. Much of Vizenor's work that has been described as postmodernist is in fact his effort to dismantle the false image of the "Indian": the European creation that dates from Columbus's "discovery" of the New World. Contemporary critical theory, particularly the writings of Jacques Derrida, Jean-François Lyotard, Jean Baudrillard, and others of the poststructuralist school of thought, is used by Vizenor not to display some putative deconstructive allegiance on his part; on the contrary, critical theory serves the interests of bringing tribal epistemologies to a contemporary readership. In an interview with A. Robert Lee, Vizenor explains his sense of the contiguity between contemporary theory and the tribal oral tradition: "The demands upon a better language of interpretation, you know, in current thought, are probably similar to demands that were once brought to oral stories. . . . The critique of language and literature today is something similar to what native storiers must have done, as they were overburdened with authority, healer dealers, and the politics of tradition in stories."[30]

Critics such as Alan Velie have used the framework of postmodernist fiction to approach Vizenor's work, especially the early fiction. In the final chapter of *Four American Indian Literary Masters* (1982), "Beyond the Novel Chippewa-Style: Gerald Vizenor's Post-Modern Fiction," Velie uses the context of the so-called new fiction of the 1970s to characterize Vizenor's writing style, specifically the style of his first novel, *Darkness in Saint Louis Bearheart*. Taking as his starting point Philip Stevick's "axioms" for a postmodern aesthetic, Velie proposes that "the new fiction ignores established fictional traditions to an extraordinary extent, purposely establishes a limited audience, departs from the illusionist tradition, and represents writing as play,"[31] that it eschews the "common reader," and that it includes plentiful reference to trashy popular or "schlock" culture. Consequently Velie reads *Bearheart* as lacking philosophical or aesthetic depth; the text rejects symbolism in favor of the aesthetics of the surface and, like postmodern fiction in general, makes no attempt to create an illusion of reality. Caricature, exaggeration, and play are placed at the center of the text's aesthetic style. However, rather than attributing these characteristics to European postmodernism, Velie argues that Vizenor's use of these textual strategies means that he "owes more of a debt to his Anishinaabe grandmother than to Hemingway or Faulkner."[32]

Vizenor himself discusses the relationship between postmodernism and tribal stories in the introduction to *Narrative Chance*. He lists four aspects of the postmodern condition that have an impact on literary narratives and on Native American writing in particular: linear time is abolished, dreams are a source of reality, every telling of a story is a new story, and there is a strong connection to oral expression. The key difference between Vizenor's list and the axioms proposed by Philip Stevick is that while Stevick treats postmodernism in terms of specific textual characteristics, Vizenor understands postmodernism as a condition rather than a creed, an experience rather than a conceptual object. Vizenor explains to Larry McCaffery and Tom Marshall, "The conditions are postmodern because of their connection to oral expression which is usually a kind of a free-floating signifier or a collection of signifiers, depending on who's present. The meaning of such stories that are orally presented depends on a number of interesting, lively, immediate, temporal, and dangerous, dangerous natural conditions."[33] By "dangerous" in this context, Vizenor means an encounter with the unknown under conditions where agreed upon and expected meanings or conventions are placed under threat of subversion or dissolution. In conversation with Laura Coltelli, Vizenor accepts the designation of his work as postmodern but with the ironic comment that he is the only contemporary native writer who accepts the reference. Even given this openness to postmodernism, he stresses that for him postmodernism is precisely as Jean-François Lyotard defined it, a condition rather than a thought or idea or a theory.[34] "The meaning is in the telling," he says, "not in the reference, but in the telling. I say that's the meaning and that's postmodern. . . . It's in the discourse and that's where the real is, that's the truth of it."[35]

The fact that Vizenor addresses the postmodern condition in which his texts are written and received does not presuppose that he is a postmodernist writer. Vizenor develops Hartwig Isernhagen's suggestion that his commitment to the idea of mystery, beneath words and in characters, which language attempts to capture, is a modernist strategy: "I am a modernist by way of the appreciation of the imagination of characters, and especially those characters with whom I have had a real experience and whom I have tried to present in fiction. . . . But when it comes to the racial binaries I am a postmodernist."[36] Vizenor nuances his use of the term "modernist" by noting that modernism's primitivism or nostalgia for the primitive carries with it notions of the universal, which would undermine his respect for imagination and the specifics of his characters.[37] Talking about his 1992 novel *The Heirs of Columbus*, Vizenor describes the world-changing power of literature in what might be called modernist (rather than postmodernist) terms when he argues that the world "can be changed with a poetic intensity, a shamanic ecstatic experience: concentration, meditation, a thoughtful attention to the peaceful healing interests of a good story, the poetic ecstatic moment, an instance of inspiration, careful and poetic attention to a condition of life, can transform it."[38] If we read the term "ecstatic" as "epiphanic," the kind of reality-changing epiphany described by modernist writers such as Virginia Woolf and James Joyce can be seen at work in Vizenor's vision of the value of literary art. However, any parallel between Vizenor's work and that of Anglo-American modernists must be qualified by the awareness that Vizenor always works within a tribal context.

In his preface to *Earthdivers: Tribal Narratives on Mixed Descent* (1981), Vizenor describes the goal of mixed-blood or métis writing as the creation of "a new consciousness of co-existence."[39] The earthdiver of myth was compelled to dive deep into the flooded world in order to find the grains of soil that would be the beginnings of a new world. Now Vizenor's contemporary métis earthdivers must "swim deep down and around through federal exclaves and colonial economic enterprises in search of a few honest words upon which to build a new urban turtle island."[40] This new world is constructed from language, out of the resources of imagination, and is based on an understanding of the fundamental nature of contingency and chance. Thus Vizenor's putative postmodernism arises from his commitment to revealing the arbitrary nature of identities that always exist in language or other representational discourses. He tells Laura Coltelli, "This is an interesting problem in life, that I can stand here but I'm not believable until I show you a photograph of myself. In the politics of passports and international recognition we don't exist unless we have a photograph showing that we exist. Standing here, in the flesh, is seldom enough. In other words, it's a simulation." But in his fiction, as he explains, Vizenor creates characters who "abolish this western dependence on simulations and restore a connection to the real, to the referent."[41] In a postmodern culture that values the representation, the simulation, a writer such as Vizenor works to connect the reader with the real and specifically with a tribal presence. In place of the artificial "Indian" of popular culture, Vizenor seeks to instantiate a real tribal subject. He describes the static condition of "invented Indians" to Neal Bowers and Charles Silet: "We're invented from traditional static standards and we are stuck in coins and words like artifacts. So we take up a belief and settle with it, stuck, static."[42]

The characteristics of Vizenor's writing most frequently described as postmodernist are the deconstructive features of his work. Vizenor's term for the work of subverting the oppressive stereotypes that trap tribal people is "socioacupuncture," the application of semantic pressure on those places that are sensitive to the absurd nature of racial and national categorization. In his essay "Socioacupuncture: Mythic Reversals and the Striptease in Four Scenes," Vizenor draws upon Roland Barthes's understanding of the striptease as a contradiction, a spectacle based on ritual and pretense. "Tribal cultures are colonized in a reversal of the striptease," he writes. "Familiar tribal images are patches on the 'pretense of fear,' and there is a sense of 'delicious terror' in the structural opposition of savagism and civilization found in the cinema and in the literature of romantic captivities. Plains tepees, and the signs of moccasins, canoes, feathers, leathers, arrowhead, numerous museum artifacts, conjure the cultural rituals of the traditional tribal past, but the pleasures of the tribal striptease are denied, data bound, stopped in emulsion, colonized in print to resolve the insecurities and inhibitions of the dominant culture."[43] The false image of native communities propagated in Hollywood movies and popular photography impose layers of imagistic pretense upon native cultures that cannot be stripped away. This is the reversal of the cultural striptease.

An important part of Vizenor's critique of false representations of native people is his exposure of the manufactured nature of Edward Curtis's famous photographs: "Curtis retouched tribal images; he, or his darkroom assistants, removed hats, labels, suspenders, parasols, from photographic prints. . . . Curtis paid some tribal people to pose for photographs; he sold their images and lectured on their culture to raise cash to continue his travels to tribal communities. He traveled with his camera to capture the neonoble tribes, to preserve metasavages in the ethnographic present as consumable objects of the past."[44] Curtis's activities constitute an early instance of what Vizenor elsewhere denounces as a "consumer renaissance" of native performances.[45] Against the false performances of native "savagery" found in Curtis's images, Vizenor contrasts the photographs taken in a reservation context in his essay "Imagic Presence: Native Pictomyths and Photographs," the foreword to Bruce White's book *We Are at Home: Pictures of the Ojibway People*, published by the Minnesota Historical Society in 2006. Vizenor likens tribal photographs to native pictomyths and totemic drawings as a source of meaning that is generated by native people themselves as opposed to images that are taken of them by outsiders. Vizenor draws attention to the fact that the Anishinaabe have always readily adopted technological innovations, and the Kodak Brownie, the cardboard box camera introduced in 1900, was no exception. The images produced by the inexpensive Brownie provide a stark contrast with the studio photographs of tribal people, which simulate images of Indians to provide postcards and other images for a white market. Vizenor reports Bruce White's comment that the studio portraits of Anishinaabe leaders taken in the 1850s placed the figures in poses that resembled European portraiture, in artificial settings characterized by clothing and accessories derived from white stereotypes of tribal people. "The studio poses were formal, often ceremonious natives and families, in sharper focus, serious, retouched poses in front of ethereal backdrops," Vizenor writes. "The box camera, however, inspired a new perception and consciousness of the real, of humans and nature, a new expressive, wondrous world of black, white, and gray eyes and hands in distinctive, arrested motion."[46] This implied motion, the arrested hand gesture, is important because it is symptomatic of the new casual approach to photography and functions as a sign of the lived presence of the figure in the image—opposed to the static and posed nature of studio portraits.

While Vizenor opposes the images that tribal people create of themselves to those marketed by European photographers, his work does not represent a simple opposition between native and nonnative. On the contrary, as A. Robert Lee in his introduction to the essay collection *Loosening the Seams: Interpretations of Gerald Vizenor* (2000) remarks, "Once subjected to Euro-American gaze, politics, power, and language, Native peoples, [Vizenor] suggests, indeed became 'othered' *avant la lettre*, their lives and histories made over into chimerae, shadows, figures of fantasy in a whole diorama of invention. . . . In consequence, there has been no hesitation in taking on conventional pieties both non-Native *and* Native. Manifest Destiny or the Winning of the West loom large, but so, too, do arbitrary notions of

Blood Quantum or Mother Earth."[47] Those Europeans who impose false racialized identities and the native people who embrace stereotypes are equally the focus of Vizenor's deconstructive or "postmodern" critique. As A. LaVonne Brown Ruoff comments, "The major thrust of Vizenor's work— whether poetry, prose, or drama—is the examination of the interrelationships between the tribal and non-tribal worlds."[48] In a postmodern era these relations are shaped by simulations that control all aspects of the relationship. In the interview with Jack Foley, Vizenor is asked, "What does it mean 'to discover an Indian'?" and he gives the following response: "To possess! The interesting key here is the idea of *simulation*. Of course, so much of post-anything life is one of simulation: photographs, images, motion pictures, the things we take pleasure in are simulations. The distinction here, though, comes from Jean Baudrillard in the work he did on simulations, where it refers to the idea that the simulation has no reference. It's just a pure invention, and then that invention becomes the real, so that you have to be suspicious of your own memory, your own experience; you have to suspend them because the power of the simulation has taken control of everything real."[49] In this copy without an original, this invention posing as the real, lies the inspiration of Vizenor's postmodernism.

The Contexts of Vizenor's Vocabulary

Vizenor sees himself as a revolutionary writer who unsettles and disrupts the status quo. His primary weapon is language. In an interview he confesses, "I see myself as being dangerously revolutionary in terms of ideas, and I edit myself often in speech and edit myself quite often in writing. I'm still educating an audience. For example, about Indian identity I have a revolutionary fervour. The hardest part of it is I believe we're all invented as Indians. . . . I consider these ideas very revolutionary because so many people have grown comfortable with the goals and offerings of the institution. People get tired; things are okay for a lot of people. I also feel the sense of esthetic revolution, too. I think writing ought to be pushing consciousness."[50] Vizenor challenges and extends the epistemological range of his reader through his innovative use of language and his distinctive vocabulary. That the reader is the focus of his linguistic style becomes clear in the following exchange with Jack Foley, which concerns Vizenor's motivation for creating his own vocabulary:

> GV: Yes, it's part of mythic re-creation; it is part of the power of a story that you must not just describe the circumstances of the story, that gives meaning to the story, but you create the presence of the experience in the story itself, and, to do that, many times you need new words or new language.

> JF: Well, particularly I think in the situation of a colonized people, a people who have been oppressed by another people. All right, I'll take that language, I'll take English; I'll use it, but I'm going to use it in a way that's different.

> GV: You come to the vocabulary that I provide for you.[51]

Vizenor suggests that although the reader's active participation in the experience of the text is central to his concern, the author is always in control of shaping that experience through the choice of words that appear on the page. In an interview with Laura Coltelli, Vizenor describes "all of us [as] prisoners of our languages."[52] He goes on to describe this condition as a consequence of translation and interpretation, noting, "We are colonial subjects of names and mostly of nouns."[53] Arguing that we are rarely victimized by verbs, Vizenor explains the importance of naming, especially in a tribal context: "Practically every tribal name is a western colonial imposition: the tribes don't speak of themselves that way, but they must, in a written language, do so. Just encountering a word is a creative act in a word war. If someone says, 'Are you an American Indian?,' you have an instant word war; all you have to do is, say no."[54] In what might be an effective summary of his entire oeuvre, Vizenor proclaims, "I refuse to accept the world the way it is especially in language. So I first encounter language and then change the world through language and imagination."[55] The deceptive power of language is both a negative and a positive force: "To counter the world with language is necessary in order to be liberated. . . . Otherwise we are dominated by the words that define us."[56]

To be defined by rather than defining the words we use, to be dominated linguistically by discourses that lead to a single absolute meaning, is to fall victim to what Vizenor calls "terminal creeds." This term appears in a 1981 interview in which Vizenor allows himself to make some admittedly generalized observations about tribal cultures and native attitudes toward the tribal ideal of balance. In contrast to the tribal view, he claims, the "Christian objective is to rid the self and the soul, the family, and the community, of evil, to isolate it and destroy it. It's a war, a holy war to end evil. The same language is a part of American consciousness—the war on poverty, the war against ignorance. The objective is completely to end and destroy it [the enemy]. But the experience expressed in tribal culture is not that complete elimination or annihilation of anything. It's a balance, not a terminal creed."[57] A terminal creed is, then, a belief that ends conflict through the definitive triumph of an absolute. Other examples of terminal creeds that adversely affect tribal people include the mourning of a "lost" tribal world, formalized as the myth of the "Vanishing American." Vizenor writes against the traumatizing, monolithic "terminal creeds" perpetuated in social science discourses; these destructive stereotypes of "primitive" tribal people are embedded in the institutional understandings of "Indianness" that Ishi, the "museum Indian," emblematizes in Vizenor's writings. These monologic Western epistemologies perpetuate trauma, and it is these that Vizenor sets out to subvert with irony, humor, and a language that refuses to render absolute monologic meanings.

In opposition to terminal creeds, Vizenor seeks in his writing to promote the concept of "survivance." He tells Isernhagen, "If we have *dominance*—in other words, a condition that's recognizable as a world view—then surely we have *survivance*, we have a condition of not being a victim."[58] Like his understanding of postmodernism, survivance is for Vizenor a condition, not an object. It is a way of thinking and acting in the world that refuses domination and the position of the victim. In *Fugitive Poses* (1998) Vizenor notes that "survivance, in the sense of native survivance, is more than survival, more than endurance or mere response; the stories of survivance are an active presence."[59] Survivance is not passive survival but active resistance as well; it is the refusal of the insistence upon tribal people as "Vanished," or as tragic victims, or as ig/noble savages caught in an unchanging past, or as the vanguard of an idealized New Age future. Chris Lalonde points out that "with his fictions [Vizenor] does what Foucault argues is what makes one insane in the eyes of the community: he crosses the boundaries of the dominant bourgeois culture in order to reveal the lies upon which it is based."[60]

As should be clear from the discussion above, paramount among the lies that Vizenor engages is the invention of a category of person known as "Indian." It is for this reason, and to draw attention to the anomalous nature of the word, that Vizenor always writes "*indian*" italicized and lowercased. He has coined the term "postindian" to define the period of time since Columbus's invention of the American "Indian," during which all people named "Indians" are more properly "postindians." In the essay "American Revolutions: Transethnic Cultures and Narratives," Vizenor explains, "The word *indian* is a convenient word, a misnomer to be sure, but it is an invented name that does not come from any native language, and does not describe or contain any aspects of traditional tribal experience and literature."[61] Indeed, in an ironic comment on the Columbian discovery narrative, Vizenor has expressed his relief that Columbus was searching for a route to India and not to Turkey—because in that latter case the tribal peoples of the Americas would be known as Turkeys rather than Indians.[62] His point is that native people bear no more relation to the category of "Indians" than they do to large domesticated fowl. In the introduction to *Native American Perspectives on Literature and History* (1994), Vizenor and Alan Velie write that "Indians have been misunderstood by others since Columbus mistook the Caribs for natives of India"[63] The concept of the Indian is a colonial invention and an artefact of the colonizing viewpoint. While native people may have come to refer to themselves as Indians, they never did so before European contact. "In Vizenor's view," A. LaVonne Brown Ruoff explains, "whites invented 'Indian' as a new identity for tribal people in order to separate them from their ancient tribal traditions. To survive this cultural genocide, tribal people responded by inventing new pan-Indian creeds, ceremonies, and customs that have blinded them and whites to their true tribal heritages. Only through the visions and dreams of tricksters and shamans can both tribal people and whites be led to the truth. Vizenor sees his literary role as that of illuminating both the sham of contemporary 'Indianness' and the power of vision and dream to restore tribal values."[64]

The figure of the "postindian," then, represents resistance and survival, native survivance beyond tragedy, victimry, and the simulations of the "*indian.*" The postindian at once exposes the lack of substance that is constitutive of the stereotype (like Baudrillard's postmodern copy without an original) but at the same time suggests something of what it is that is missing. In *Manifest Manners* (1994) Vizenor explains that tribal "stories of creation, sense of imagic presence, visionary memories, and tricky survivance are the eternal traces of native modernity. . . . Native stories are an imagic presence, the actual tease of human contingencies, but *indians* are immovable simulations, the tragic archives of dominance and victimry."[65] So tribal people today, five centuries after Columbus, are those who "come after" and thus are "post" the "Indians" that Columbus created. The cause that is served by the artificial category of the "Indian" is what Vizenor calls "manifest manners," "manifest" referring to cultural dominance and "manners" to the assumption or behavior that claims dominance as destiny. "Surely most people have a general understanding, at least from the movies, that some adventurous destiny, cruel and unusual, ended out west, and out back, and now we have a nation of casinos, manifest manners, and affirmative action," Vizenor explains. "The manifest has been revised, but the notions of an originary national history are the new manners of destiny."[66] So the assumption that European settlers should dominate the landscape and the cultural mindscape of the Americas is enacted in the everyday behavior that Vizenor calls "manifest manners." "Socioacupuncture" is

Vizenor's word to describe the process of deconstructing this attitude of manifest manners: "Focusing just the right cultural pressure and mediation on the simulations of natives invites the ambiguities of association and meaning. So applying just the right socioacupuncture at the right time can, in stories, heal and liberate."[67]

Vizenor's writing in prose is often associated with the liberating figure of the tribal trickster. In the novel *Griever: An American Monkey King in China*, Vizenor emphasizes the parallels between the Chinese trickster monkey and the trickster of Anishinaabe mythology. As Alan Velie observes, "Vizenor's conception of the trickster seems to be in line with Chippewa tradition—tricksters are benevolent but amoral, lustful, irresponsible, and given to fighting evil with trickery."[68] However, the term Vizenor most frequently associates with the Anishinaabe woodland trickster, Naanabozho, is "compassionate."[69]

It is important to keep in mind, however, that for Vizenor the trickster is not so much a character as a way of thinking, speaking, and acting. The linguistic nature of the trickster figure is emphasized in Vizenor's work. The trickster, Vizenor explains, is not a person but a force within language:

> This is the condition of most trickster stories: they do anything, they confront everyone, they do the most outrageous, transformational, exploitative, contradictory things that end up with nothing. No advantage, no political game; trickster ends up with nothing, and that's what it is, it's a liberation. If a trickster ended up with something in a story, he would then be representational, he would be more like a human, therefore having human motivations and becoming suspect. If a trickster were representational you would be able to challenge everything trickster did, according to

representational values. The trickster plays on the edge of metaphor, he is not representational; he plays out all of the metaphors of embellishment, exaggeration and human encounter, and does anything transformational. . . . This is important in a story, otherwise it wouldn't have this kind of sense of liberation; that it's all language play, it's not representational.[70]

If the trickster was simply represented as a "real" human person in the story, the trickster's achievements could be explained in terms of human motives such as power or greed. But Vizenor is interested in opening new possibilities for seeing the world and transforming it through compassion, of finding a way to reconstruct our discursive relations so we can live with greater fairness and justice.

This does not mean that the trickster resolves conflict; on the contrary, he holds in balance warring sides and makes it possible to live in the state of uncertainty that results. For example, a story to which Vizenor returns in his writing concerns Naanabozho's challenge to the evil Gambler of Anishinaabe myth. Naanabozho will save the souls of the people if he wins the gamble; if he loses then the Gambler receives the scalps, ears, and hands of his victims, the bodies will be given to the *wiindigoo* or cannibals, and the spirits will be consigned to *niibaagiizis*, the land of darkness. He must throw a dish containing four human figures, representing the four ages of man, in such a way that the figures all land standing up. Naanabozho does this and, as the Gambler throws the dish, the trickster makes a strange whistling noise that causes the Gambler to move and the figures to fall. Thus Naanabozho wins—but he wins only this one time, and the story suggests that the people will in the future again be threatened by the Gambler. Evil does not disappear; Naanabozho makes it possible for the people to live with the knowledge of evil and in the presence of danger. The trickster takes on simplistic single meanings and all forms of semantic closure, such as those found in terminal creeds, or what Vizenor calls "the terminal vernacular of manifest manners, and the final vocabularies of dominance."[71] As an ironic consequence of this resistance to fixity, despite the appearance of the trickster Naanabozho in many tribal stories and myths, there can be no tradition of trickster writing because the trickster figure is hostile toward everything that constitutes a fixed and static tradition. A trickster tradition, Vizenor comments, "would be an ironic tease and a natural contradiction. Tradition, as you know, is a tamer, not a liberator."[72] Trickster narratives can be a practice or an experience but never a tradition.

The trickster thrives on the operations of "chance," another key word in Vizenor's vocabulary. In his autobiographical writings Vizenor stresses the role of chance in shaping his life: the chance encounter between his parents and his mother's chance invocation of the Hollywood movie star George Raft when she first saw Clement Vizenor; his chance encounter with Japan when his troop ship was diverted from Korea to Yokohama, from whence troops were transported by military flights to Korea (but because Vizenor's name occurs at the end of the alphabet, the flights had ceased before his turn was reached); or the offer of his first academic post from the head of department who had happened to read and like Vizenor's haiku poetry. In Vizenor's terms all of these events are evidence of the workings of chance in his life: "George Raft was the chance of my conception. Japan was my chance at the end of the alphabet, and haiku was a second chance at Lake Forest College."[73]

While chance can be a productive force, both in life and in literary narratives, Vizenor is very critical of the recent phenomenon of Indian casinos, and he makes a careful distinction between kinds of gaming. Games of chance lie at the heart of Anishinaabe tribal mythology—as in the story of the evil Gambler. Vizenor observes the difference between games that are set to favor the house, so that the gambler will always ultimately lose, and games of genuine chance such as bingo. In his 1992 editorial comment, published in *American Indian Quarterly*, Vizenor explains that the Indian Gaming Regulatory Act of 1988 "recognized that the tribes have the 'exclusive right to regulate gaming' if the activity is not prohibited by federal or state laws. . . . The new law established three classes of gaming: the first, traditional tribal games; the second, games such as bingo, lotto, and pulltabs; the third, and the most controversial of the classes, includes lotteries, slot machines, blackjack, parimutuel betting, and other casino games."[74] In his editorial Vizenor frames this information with the story of Luther Standing Bear, who in his autobiography tells how the train taking him to Carlisle Indian School in Pennsylvania stopped briefly in Sioux City. White people approached the train, throwing money at the young Indian travelers. Standing Bear reports that the boys were warned by one of their group not to keep the money but to throw it back—at which point the white people laughed and threw more. Vizenor creates a parallel between this historical episode and the contemporary situation where white people "throw money" at Indians via reservation casinos but now Indians give nothing of this money back in state fees or taxes. This has serious implications for native sovereignty, as Vizenor points out: "Congress . . . negotiated treaties with the tribes and has the absolute power to terminate reservations."[75] By this he means that the plenary power of Congress encompasses this capacity to terminate reservations. He suggests an alternative to "the unresolved issues of state taxation and the enforcement of criminal statutes on reservations [that] could cause more contention between the tribes and state governments." In Vizenor's view tribes could establish for themselves sovereign international standing by establishing embassies abroad and by offering asylum to stateless families: "The liberation of Kurdish, Tibetan, Haitian, and other families, for instance, would sustain the moral traditions of tribal cultures. The relocation of these families to reservation communities would situate an undeniable tribal sovereignty, and earn international eminence."[76] In his novel *The Heirs of Columbus*, Vizenor explores this idea of the reservation as a place of asylum for refugees both domestic and from abroad.

Despite the dangers that can arise from abuses of the power of chance, Vizenor recognizes that the wealth generated first by bingo and then by casinos has been a positive development in some tribal communities. Acknowledging that there is always the danger of corruption, Vizenor points to the use of this money to "do such pragmatic things as construct buildings, pave roads, lay sewage lines, improve their water supply." He continues, "This is very pragmatic. You would think that the federal government might have been able to figure it out after a couple of hundred years. Bingo did what the federal government hasn't been able to do for a century, and I'm not sure exactly how to interpret this in the course of history; maybe politics isn't capable of a good gamble."[77] The power of chance underlies this "course of history," bringing pragmatic improvements in the lives of tribal people. The transformative power of chance is a positive force in Vizenor's work, where sites of transformation acquire particular significance: portals and thresholds; solstices, equinoxes, dawns, and dusks; state and international borders; and change and inheritance through heirship all are very powerful aspects of Vizenor's work.

Perhaps the single most empowering characteristic that appears in Vizenor's writing is what he calls "crossblood" or "mixedblood" identities. Vizenor's contemporary urban "earthdivers"—the creators of new discursive worlds—are métis, the mixed-blood descendants of tribal people and European settlers in New France. In "Crows Written on the Poplars: Autocritical Autobiographies," he writes that "mixedbloods loosen the seams in the shrouds of identities," and when asked about this image, he explained to A. Robert Lee that "the irony here, the cultural irony, is that the seams are simulations of dominance. The seams are sewn over and over by social scientists and other inventors of the American Indian. And the invention is a conservative, national allegory of cultural difference and distinction."[78] The mixed-blood person has then the power to expose the constructed nature of "Indian" identity, to prove the difference between blood and culture. "This is a difficult issue because of the complication of the racial politics of the United States which treats Native Americans differently to other ethnic groups," Vizenor explains to Laura Coltelli. He points out that when an African American marries a white person, their offspring remain African American; however, when "Indians intermarry, they instantly become white. They stop being Indian in the racialism of American consciousness, and at the same time, whites forever pretend to be Indian."[79] Vizenor's own mixed background is vitally important to his sense of himself as a writer and thinker: "If you ask me to characterize my work in a few words I could say that I'm encountering a mixedblood experience in a creative way, to give consciousness to crossblood experience, to create a consciousness of crossblood identity. This is a confrontation in so many ways; it's an international confrontation, it's a confrontation of American racialism because of the genetic categories of who's Indian, and I'll not allow the world to deny my experience just to fulfill some genetic category."[80]

CHAPTER 2

Gerald Vizenor as Journalist, Tribal Historian, and Cultural Critic

It is very difficult to separate the fictional from the documentary in Vizenor's work. Even on the level of characterization, Vizenor freely mixes historical figures with those of pure imagination. When asked about this aspect of his writing, Vizenor has described his style as "narrative faction . . . fictive journalism, something like that" and cites the preface to the first edition of his novel *Bearheart*, which "announced that the real names in the novel were not, and the imagined characters were real."[1] So the imaginary is real and the real is fictional. This playing with ontology, which forces the reader to speculate about what is real and why it is thought of as real, is entirely characteristic of all Vizenor's work. In an interview with Kimberly Blaeser, Vizenor comments on the way he has fictionalized his experience in books such as *Wordarrows*, *Earthdivers*, and *Crossbloods*, especially his activities and encounters as a community organizer: "It exceeds fiction. People wouldn't believe that if it were fiction."[2] The Anishinaabe quality of Vizenor's writing contributes to the significant overlap between fictive and historical writing; as he remarks in *The Everlasting Sky: New Voices from the People Named the Chippewa*, "The *oshki anishinabe* writer tells stories now as in the past—stories about people not facts."[3] Vizenor,

true to this tradition, tells stories about people. Despite his delib-
erate confusion of fiction and fact, this chapter deals with Vizenor's documentary work in separation from his novels, which
are discussed in chapter 5. The separation is necessary because
although Vizenor plays with stylistic assumptions about the real
and the imagined, there are important differences of genre,
intent, and form as a consequence of which the documentary
work requires separate consideration. And while Vizenor's novels have received a great deal of critical attention, this is not the
case with his historical and journalistic writings, which are more
often used together with his cultural commentary justifiably to
illuminate aspects of his novels.

Among Vizenor's earliest publications there appeared, both
in 1970, the paired books *Anishinabe nagamon: Songs of the
People* and *Anishinabe adisokan: Tales of the People. Anishinabe nagamon* is a second paperback edition of *Summer in
the Spring: Lyric Poems of the Ojibway*, which first appeared
in a limited hardbound edition. This book is a collection
of Vizenor's interpretations of traditional Anishinaabe songs
based on Frances Densmore's translations. *Anishinabe adisokan* consists of traditional Anishinaabe narratives that were
originally translated and published between December 1887
and May 1888 in the *Progress*, the White Earth Reservation
newspaper edited by Vizenor's great uncle, Theodore Hudon
Beaulieu. The stories were originally recounted in *anishinaabemowin* (the Anishinaabe language) by two members of the
sacred *midewiwin*, Day Dodge and Saycosegay; Theodore
Beaulieu translated the stories and published them under his
name. The book then sets out several myths that are central to
Vizenor's work: the origin of the *midewiwin* ceremony (which
explains why Vizenor makes frequent references to bears, to

cedar, and the task of Naanabozho the trickster hero), the myth of the evil Gambler, the earthdiver myth, and the story of the origin of the Anishinaabeg, which Vizenor tells in the opening section of *The People Named the Chippewa*. A third edition of the poems and second edition of the stories appeared as *Summer in the Spring: Ojibwe Lyric Poems and Tribal Stories* (1981) and was reprinted as *Summer in the Spring: Anishinaabe Lyric Poems and Stories* (1981).

Summer in the Spring is divided into two sections, the first comprising poems and the second stories. Most of the poems and stories are accompanied by tribal pictomyths. Throughout Vizenor is concerned to restore a sense of the oral origins of the written texts. He includes words in *anishinaabemowin* italicized and in lowercase, deliberately rejecting the grammatical and punctuation conventions of written English. As he explains in the section "Interpretive Notes": "The cultural and political histories of the *anishinaabeg* were written in the language of those who invented the *indian*, renamed the tribes, allotted the land, divided ancestry by geometric designs and categorized identity by colonial reservations."[4] In his introduction to the book, Vizenor begins by emphasizing the transition from the spoken to the written that the text represents. He reminds us that tribal communities had no need of written languages and translations. "The translations and interpretations in this collection," he notes, "are the remembered shadows of the heard visions and stories of tribal survivance" (4). Thus the original stories and dream songs enacted a sense of tribal presence to which written texts can only gesture.

The related issues of language and the invented nature of "*indians*" are taken up in Vizenor's foreword and introduction to *The Everlasting Sky: New Voices from the People Named the*

Chippewa (1972). In the foreword he explains that the name "Anishinaabe" is the word by which tribal people called themselves before the imposition of colonial names such a "Chippewa." This name, Anishinaabe, referred to the families that formed the basic economic and social unit, providing both personal and group identity. Consequently Vizenor uses the term "*anishinabe*" to refer to the people of the tribal past and "*oshki anishinabe*" to name "the new people of the woodland of today."[5] As in *Summer in the Spring*, these terms are italicized and lowercased. The introduction continues this theme, opening with an invitation to write a short definition of the word "indian" to which the reader can return "as you read and listen to the *oshki anishinabe* . . . expressing their anger and dreams and fears" (xiii). The attentive reader, Vizenor suggests, will finally abandon the concept of the *indian,* "erase the whole idea of the *indian* in the mind—respecting the unique cultural diversity of the *oshki anishinabe* of today" (xiii–xiv). The pieces that comprise the book derive from various sources. "The Four Ages of Man" is a lengthier retelling of the story of Naanabozho and the evil Gambler that appeared in *Summer in the Spring* and was first published in the *Progress.* Many of the other pieces are broadly autobiographical, based on memories of Vizenor's encounters with tribal people both on reservations and in the city.

As these two introductory essays indicate, Vizenor has written this book for nontribal readers who have yet to appreciate the living diversity of Native Americans in general and of the Anishinaabe in particular. So a further introductory chapter, "The Woodland Reservations," consists of a factual account of the six Anishinaabe reservations in the state of Minnesota with a brief history of each that stresses the extent to which original treaty lands have passed out of tribal ownership since the mid–nineteenth century. This loss of land provides an important context for the stories of the *oshki anishinabe* that follow, such as "The People are Afraid of Change," which addresses reservation politics and the effect on tribal people of a history of white promises of change that in fact have meant the loss of tribal land. A second important context is established by the story "The Four Ages of Man," which begins with the words of his grandmother spoken to Naanabozho: "My grandson, the land which you intend to visit is infested with many evil spirits and the followers of those who eat human flesh. . . . No one who has ever been within their power has ever been known to return" (1). The parallel between Naanabozho's encounter with the Gambler and the *oshki anishinabe* experience in the dominant American culture provides an interpretive framework for the stories that follow. The book is introduced in a complex way that offers various aspects of tribal experience. The formal introductory material is presented in the foreword and introduction, but before we reach the title page of "The Everlasting Sky" we read the introductory history of the Minnesota reservations and then, when we think we have reached the first story, about Naanabozho, this also proves to be introductory. Only after reading four stories— one mythical, one historical, one that addresses the point of view of the reader and the other the perspective of the author—do we finally begin to engage with the book proper. This complicated introduction allows Vizenor to present the book as a collection of survivance stories: the guiding spirit is perhaps Naanabozho who was challenged by the Gambler and tricked his way to winning but the stories also express the tragic losses experienced by the Anishinaabe people.

To tell stories of police brutality, of injustice before the law, and of housing that is, as the title of one story indicates, "Little

More than an Inside Toilet" without victimry is the challenge Vizenor meets in this book as elsewhere. These stories include "The Sacred Names Were Changed," which tells how the "woodland identity of the people was homogenized in patent histories" (7) and the name "*indian*"; "Something the White Man Named," which describes individual struggles with the word "*indian*," which, as the narrator comments, "is a heavy burden to the *oshki anishinabe* because white people know more about the *indian* they invented than anyone" (15–16); the following piece, "Daydreaming in a White School," which concerns the suicide of a young *oshki anishinabe* girl and the role of education in propagating the destructive identity category of "*indian*" and efforts to reform curricula and pedagogy to meet the needs of tribal children; "Making It Off the Reservation," which tells the stories of tribal men whose athletic skills offered recognition in the dominant society; and "Keeping the Family Together," which addresses the role of the tribal family and the importance of women who sustain the family unit. In "Dreams in the Fourth Dimension," Vizenor writes of Ted Mahto—a poet, teacher, and school administrator—whose poem "Uncle Tomahawk" (which Vizenor reproduces in the essay) is a powerful critique of the violent socialization of "*indians*" into white society. Through the figure of Ted Mahto, Vizenor describes Anishinaabe storytelling: "Stories are a circle of believable dreams and oratorical gestures showing the meaning between the present and the past in the life of the people. The stories change as the people change because people, not facts, are the center of the anishinabe world" (69). The emphasis upon the importance of dreams and visual thinking characterizes all of Vizenor's writing.

The final story, "Buried in a Blue Suit," is reprinted in the section "Tribal Scenes and Poetic Images" in *Tribal Scenes and Ceremonies* (1976) and appears in a revised version in *The People Named the Chippewa* (1984). A. LaVonne Brown Ruoff, in her essay "Woodland Word Warrior," remarks on Vizenor's portraits of historical individuals such as John Ka Ka Geesick, whose translated name, she remarks, provided the name for Vizenor's book *The Everlasting Sky*. Vizenor has recently returned to this tribal figure in the essays collected in *Literary Chance* (2007) and to the story, which Ruoff summarizes as follows: "Ka Ka Geesick was both humiliated and immortalized by a white society that dressed him in a blue suit, turkey feather headdress, and a green blanket for an official souvenir postcard photograph and, after his death at age 124, insisted that he be buried in the same suit and given a Christian funeral service."[6] In his long life Ka Ka Geesick saw the establishment of the state of Minnesota, the reservations, and the white town that tried to transform him into an *indian* but only superficially succeeded.

Stories of people, not facts, also constitute *Wordarrows: Indians and Whites in the New Fur Trade* (1978). Many of the pieces focus on Vizenor's experiences as a community advocate and organizer in the "urban reservation" centered on Franklin Street in Minneapolis. He tells Hartwig Isernhagen that "the only fictional aspects in that book are the ways in which their stories are told and their names are changed. All of those stories came out of the tragic wisdom of human beings I know and who struggled to gain some meaning in a difficult moment in their lives."[7] Vizenor offers the example of Laurel Hole in the Day, the woman who cannot speak because she knows that if she cannot be understood one more time she will give in to despair, and Ben, who stuttered incomprehensibly because he was trying to tell everything at once and so could not be understood by police, judge, or authorities.[8] In these stories Vizenor focuses upon the cultural "word wars": "The arrowmakers and wordmakers survive the word wars with sacred memories while the factors in the new fur trade separate themselves in wordless and eventless social and political categories."[9] A. LaVonne Brown Ruoff remarks of the stories included in the section titled "Downtown on the Reservation" that they "effectively chronicle the word wars between tribal people and the dominant society."[10]

In *Wordarrows* Vizenor creates a persona, named Clement Beaulieu after his great-uncle, in order to avoid using the first-person pronoun and to connect himself to his tribal family and tribal context: "I choose that name to avoid the first person pronoun so that the me of my stories is connected to my native family. Many of my stories are not about me but about my experiences, and my activities and experiences were never separations in a pronoun. . . . Clement Beaulieu was a great storier and he is on the page with me. My persona creates a presence, not a possession. You see, the author, his persona, and his relatives are with me in the book."[11] In that last sentence Vizenor creates a distinction between "me" and "the author" that extends his observation, made in the same interview, that the use of the word "I" encourages readers to transfer their own sense of self-presence to the authorial point of view. But Vizenor is also gesturing toward the theoretical concept of the "death of the author," made popular by the French structuralist theorist Roland Barthes, where the "I" who creates the literary text ceases to be identical with the author at the moment when language takes the dominant role in determining the meaning of the text. So the "Gerald Vizenor" who wrote *Father Meme* in 2008 is not the same "Gerald Vizenor" who published *Wordarrows* in 1978, and Vizenor claims this difference by resisting the first-person pronoun, by using masks or personae, and by mediating his stories through various levels of narrative framing.

Vizenor uses the persona of Clement Beaulieu in *Earthdivers: Tribal Narratives on Mixed Descent* (1981); he uses this narrative voice to particular effect in the story "Sand Creek Survivors." As the title suggests, Vizenor juxtaposes the massacre of native people, including children, with the story of Dane Michael White, a thirteen-year-old native boy who killed himself in a Minnesota jail after forty-one days of near-solitary confinement. Dane Michael White was refused permission to live with his tribal grandmother as he wished, but the court that denied his request did not know where to place him. Later, police authorities did not know what to do with him as a runaway and so he was imprisoned. Here we can see a parallel with the figure of Ishi (discussed at length in chapter 4), who was the last tribal survivor of genocide in nineteenth-century California. When Ishi was discovered, hiding in a slaughterhouse, the police were called and, unable to think of any alternative, they placed Ishi in jail. He was "rescued" by anthropologist Alfred Kroeber and taken to live in the anthropological museum at the University of California at Berkeley. Vizenor's various tellings of this story always underline the irony that Ishi was rescued from one prison only to be placed in another. But Dane's case is complicated; as Vizenor explains in *Postindian Conversations*, "The sheriff in this case was the good guy, because it was the boy's *indian* father who insisted that his son be held in jail to teach him a lesson."[12]

The story in *Earthdivers* concerns Clement Beaulieu, the native journalist who has been sent to report on the funeral. Beaulieu's thoughts juxtapose images of tribal children speared on military bayonets with Dane White, who is metaphorically mutilated by the "funeral words" uttered by the "white institutions" that bury him. The coffin is closed so that the bruises on Dane's thirteen-year-old neck will not enter into living memory, and Clement tells himself: "We should pull these words down, beat them on altars until the truth is revealed, beat the sweet phrases from the institutions that have disguised the horrors of racism . . . drive the word pains and agonies of the heart into the cold. . . . We are the victims of these words used to cover the political violence and white horrors in the memories of the tribes. . . . Hear these primal screams, the tribes scream with the trees and rivers, from diseases, the massacres and mutilations of the heart. . . . racist isolation and the repression of the heart in white schools and institutions. . . . Break down the white word walls and dance free from isolation . . . dance in the sun."[13] In important ways these words describe Vizenor's project in his historical writings, his journalism, and his cultural commentary. They describe his efforts as a community organizer and advocate. And emphasized by the persona of Clement Beaulieu, these words describe Vizenor's tribal family legacy.

The truth that Beaulieu beats from these images is the remembered truth of genocide: the massacre of Blackfeet people at Marias Creek, the Wounded Knee Massacre, and the ongoing massacre of native children such as Dane White. But he cannot report these words in the story he telephones to his editor. The newspaper is a powerful player in what Vizenor calls the "word wars": the ongoing conflict over how history is interpreted and transmitted. Clement Beaulieu reflects, "Politicians are still keeping the world safe with words rather than guns for white settlers."[14] But finally the isolation in which Dane lived and died gives way to Beaulieu's thought that "he is not now separated from our memories and the memories of the tribal 'caretakers of the lands.'"[15] This story raises key issues of memory and story-telling. While "white words" falsify history by separating events into a linear chronology, tribal memory rejects linearity and is able to sustain the past as a living event in the present moment. "Dane White and the Sand Creek Massacre in Colorado are three generations apart in calendar time," Vizenor writes, "but in dreams and visual tribal memories, these grievous events . . . are not separated in linear time. The past can be found on tribal faces in the present. The curse of racism rules the ruinous insti-tutions and federal enclaves where tribal people are contained; where tribal blood is measured on colonial reservations. Dane White became a criminal for being truant from a white school."[16] This understanding of tribal time recurs in the piece in the final section of *Earthdivers*, "Spacious Treeline in the Woods." Here Vizenor presents the tribal oral tradition as a "visual event" that is opposed to the "grammatical time" used by nontribal translators who are engaged in "fabricating their words in prestressed phrases" that imprison imagination in "word castles."[17]

LaVonne Brown Ruoff has observed how "Vizenor's descrip-tions of the cultural wars ring true because he accurately depicts both the underlying causes of these wars and the nature of the wounds suffered by tribal people. Many of these wounds are self-inflicted, as Vizenor makes clear."[18] She gives as represen-tative examples of this self-destructiveness two stories: "The Sociodowser," in which Father Bearald One, the fake priest, is summoned to locate two stolen tribal vans that had been pur-chased with federal funds to transport tribal enrollees to a spe-cial educational program but were in fact "used for personal business most of the time" to transport tribal people to bingo games—so "the cash flowed unaccounted, ironies overburdened the games, taxes on bingo profits went unpaid, chance failed, and the red limousines were impounded" (142)—and then stolen back; and Ruoff also highlights Vizenor's satirical treatment of the blood-quantum issue in "The Chair of Tears," in which he "all too accurately depicts the administrative and student pressures that have led to the destruction of many such departments [as the fictional 'Department of Tribal Studies']."[19]

Vizenor's treatment of the complex constructions of the Anishinaabeg continues in *The People Named the Chippewa: Narrative Histories* (1984), in which he engages with the work of early writers such as William Whipple Warren, George Copway (Kahgegagahbowh), and Peter Jones (Kahkewaquonaby) as well as the *oshki anishinabe* of the American Indian Movement (AIM). Linda Ainsworth, in her essay "History and the Imagination: Gerald Vizenor's *The People Named the Chippewa*," describes how Vizenor "challenges on two fronts, first that his own Chippewa are to be identified with the Indians who populate American history textbooks, and second that the continuance of Chippewa culture rests on adherence to a set of inflexible rules governing behavior. . . . To do so, Vizenor turns to what has been most long-lived among his own Chippewa: he looks to the oral storytelling tradition. There he finds not the repository of tribal traditions that can be reconstructed whole, without change, in the present, but evidence that something vital has never been lost."[20] The most prominent example of this tribal continuance, as Ainsworth notes, is tribal identity through storytelling and the freedom of self-imagination that this cultural creativity promotes. The importance of telling oneself who one is, of tribal self-creation and self-expression, is the reason Vizenor is so critical of anthropological, ethnographic, and other social science methodologies. He notes that "anthropologists and historians invent tribal cultures and end mythic time. The differences between tribal imagination and social scientific invention are determined in world views: imagination is a state of being, a measure of personal courage; the invention of cultures is a material achievement through objective methodologies. To imagine the world is to be in the world; to invent the world with academic predications is to separate human experiences from the world, a secular transcendence and denial of chance and mortalities."[21] In *Earthdivers: Tribal Narratives on Mixed Descent* (1981), Vizenor offers a more scatological critique of anthropologists. He moves from a brief account of the fecal interpretation given the earthdiver myth to the following observation: "The creation myth that anthropologists never seem to tell is the one where *naanabozho*, the cultural trickster, made the first anthropologist from fecal matter. Once made, more were cloned in graduate schools from the first fecal creation of an anthropologist."[22] Vizenor argues that social scientists treat tribal stories as representative artifacts rather than as what Vizenor calls "figuration, because they're not literary artists. They're methodologists looking for objects to represent, a faux reality."[23]

In *The People Named the Chippewa*, Vizenor returns to the figure of Dennis Banks; his essay "Dennis of Wounded Knee," which first appeared in *American Indian Quarterly*, is reprinted in this book. Ruoff observes that if a figure such as Dane Michael White or Thomas White Hawk (discussed below) represents the tragedy of "cultural schizophrenia," then Dennis Banks represents the comedy.[24] In *Tribal Scenes and Ceremonies* (1976), Vizenor devotes to the American Indian Movement a section that comprises six pieces that originally appeared in the *Minneapolis Tribune* in March 1973: "Confrontation Heroes,"

"Killing Indians in South Dakota," "Bandits in Rapid City," "Good Little Indians Too Long," "Racism on Frontier Circle," and "Urban Militants on Reservations." What emerges from these editorial pieces is a sense of the real conditions of poverty, social injustice, and cultural alienation suffered by tribal people twinned with the complexities of effective militant action. One of Vizenor's earliest autobiographical works, "I Know What You Mean, Erdupps MacChurbbs," features a section titled "1972. We Came Here to Die" in which Vizenor tells the story of the urban AIM warriors encountering Simon Howard, then president of the Minnesota Chippewa Tribe, in a reservation classroom where they must sit on "little-people chairs," a context that subverts their militaristic rhetoric.[25] The story is repeated in *Postindian Conversations*. In the editorial "Confrontation Heroes," reprinted in *Tribal Scenes and Ceremonies*, Vizenor contrasts the changes brought about through negotiation with the confrontational strategies used by the militants of AIM. The agreement reached over hunting and fishing rights was ratified by the state legislature and was worth half a million dollars per year to the reservation. Vizenor wryly observes, "Many militants stated then that they had come to Cass Lake to die for tribal people. The issue was won through the courts, and suicide was not necessary."[26] This ironic comment is symptomatic of a characteristic noted by Robert Silberman: "Vizenor's early work was marked by a split arising from a journalistic style that seemed uncomfortable with its supposed neutrality, both because of its passion and because Vizenor's voice seemed unable to attune itself to the bland formulations of journalistic 'objectivity'; it was always being intruded upon—in wonderful ways—by a sensitive, poetic strain that shaped itself into images, by a passionate, polemical side that led to fierce ironies, slashing statements."[27]

Earlier than the editorials for the *Minneapolis Tribune*, Vizenor wrote the lengthy pamphlet *Thomas James White Hawk* (1968), which was reprinted in *Tribal Scenes and Ceremonies*. Vizenor's account of White Hawk's crime, sentencing, and commutation is told in two stories, "Murder on Good Friday" and "Commutation of Death." There is no attempt to evade the violent crime of which White Hawk was accused. The first story is further divided into a number of vignettes. After a description of the known events leading to and after the murder, Vizenor turns to "The Hearing," then to a portrait of "Little Tom White Hawk," then to "The Arraignment," "Jail Time," "The Trial," "The Head Injury," "The Psychiatrists," "The Stands Trial," "The Sentence," and "The Aftermath." This story was published in *Twin Citian Magazine* in June 1968; "Commutation of Death," consisting of a single short section, appeared in the same magazine in January 1970. The text is illustrated with photographs of the main actors in this drama—the judge, the attorneys, the accused and his accomplice, but not the victims—and the setting, Vermillion, South Dakota. Vizenor tells the story in minute detail, including such circumstantial information as "Clay County Sheriff Arnold Nelson had been trying all week to get his hair cut before Easter Sunday."[28] This attention to detail on the part of the journalist sets into ironic contrast the failure of medical and legal authorities to take account of the fact that White Hawk had suffered a serious head injury that left him with substantial disabilities such as excruciating headaches, shortness of temper, dizziness, and lapses of memory. The latter is especially significant in relation to his inability to account for the events surrounding the killing of James Yeado and his part in those events. The particular experience of Thomas White Hawk as an orphaned tribal boy who may have been suffering what Vizenor calls "cultural schizophrenia" is not taken into account at any point in his arrest, imprisonment, trial, and sentencing. Vizenor agrees with Isernhagen that the factual editorial pieces represent a situation in which single notions of justice no longer work.[29] "This is an elusive and difficult case," he reflects, "and everyone around it could not understand the crime. Those people needed this bright young man, needed their bright Indian; that's what my stories are about. So much of the Native world is unnameable. Violence, silence, and the unnameable."[30]

With some revision this text was reprinted in *Crossbloods: Bone Courts, Bingo, and Other Reports* (1990) under the section heading "Capital Punishment," with photographs of South Dakota governor Frank Farrar, a uniformed Thomas White Hawk at Shattuck School, and his guardian Philip Zoubeck replacing the single photograph of Douglas Hall with Thomas's uncle Charles White Hawk that appears in *Tribal Scenes and Ceremonies*. The story is told differently in "White Hawk and the Prairie Fun Dancers," the concluding section of *Word-arrows: Native States of Literary Sovereignty* (2003). The first three stories, "No Rest for the Good Sheriff," "Daisie and Beacher on the Prairie," "Word War in the Partsroom," and "Prosecutors and Prairie Fun Dancers," are organized around Clement Beaulieu's interviews with the main protagonists, though not Thomas White Hawk: Sheriff Arnold Nelson, who is asked about the attempted lynching of White Hawk while he was being held in Clay County jail; Reverend Beacher Givens and his wife Daisie, who are asked about their relationship with White Hawk and Daisie's emotionally charged visits with him in jail; and James Yeado's friends and pallbearers, who are more concerned to accuse Clement of being a communist because of his interest in justice for tribal people than to talk about their dead friend. The final section reports Clement Beaulieu's experience of White Hawk's commutation hearing. In a discussion with Isernhagen about his treatment of White Hawk, Vizenor explains that "those . . . stories that are in *Wordarrows* were . . . stories that I could not tell factually, so I had to fictionalize them."[31] The persona of Clement Beaulieu allows Vizenor to move among the various stories, to show characters other than White Hawk revealing their own crimes. The fictional work in this way takes the form of "advocacy against capital punishment."[32]

In his volumes of critical and cultural commentary, Vizenor is able to move away from the conventions of journalistic prose writing to a style that approaches more closely his fictional or novelistic mode of expression. As Juana María Rodríguez remarks, "In *Manifest Manners*, Vizenor delves deeper into the interpretive possibilities for critical theory without the burdens of journalistic simulations. His capacity for irony, word play, and theoretical imaginings are unleashed in this text."[33] The playful yet serious tone of the book is established by the cover of *Manifest Manners*, which features Andy Warhol's silk-screen portrait of Russell Means, captioned "This is not an Indian." Vizenor is clearly referencing Magritte's painting *The Treachery of Images (This Is Not a Pipe)* in order to focus attention on the figurative quality of the image, which so often is mistaken for, or confused with, the real. There are no "real" Indians, only stereotypes and images representing what colonialism would have native people be. As we have seen, this is what Vizenor refers to as the "*indian*" or as the simulation of the Indian. Vizenor points out the double attraction of this Warhol image for him: "Clearly the stoical image of the warrior is one simulation, and the other ironic simulation is that the actual artistic production of the silk screen was only supervised by Andy Warhol. Means, the warrior image, is teased by the absence of the artist and natives."[34] These artificial images of "Indians" that never existed are not only promoted by "manifest manners," but these "manners" require that manufactured simulations take the place of real living native people. According to Vizenor, "Manifest manners court the *authentic* evidence of absence, the romance of ethnic dioramas and cultural simulations."[35] Thus the discourse of native authenticity is necessary to sustain the illusion that *indians* are real while tribal people and their cultures are rendered mute and invisible. The notion of a modern tribal person contradicts the stereotype of the "*indian*" to the point where a "modern native" person becomes a contradiction in terms within the framework of "manifest manners." In this connection Vizenor again indicts ethnologists and anthropologists, who contribute materially to the dominant cultural assumption that tribal people are necessarily located in the past; however, he also highlights the survivance with which tribal people have risen to this challenge: "Native American Indians have endured the lies and wicked burdens of discoveries, the puritanical destinies of monotheism, manifest manners and simulated realities of dominance, with silence, traces of natural reason, trickster hermeneutics, the interpretation of tribal figures, and the solace of heard stories."[36]

One form of survivance is what Vizenor calls, in his book of the same name, "fugitive poses." The subtitle, *Native American Indian Scenes of Absence and Presence*, gives an indication of what Vizenor means by this term: The absence of "indians" from history has been used by some who have "turned that absence into a fugitive pose."[37] Real and present tribal people have created out of absence, the impossible stereotypes of the *indian* who never existed, an identity under cover of which they can live on their own terms. The absence of the *indian* is the simulation's lack of a referent; the presence of the native is the reference to tribal heritage and "a personal sense of presence in the world" (19): endurance, survival, and resistance. The six essays of this collection began as the Abraham Lincoln Lectures at the University of Nebraska. The first essay, "Penenative Rumors," treats the native essay and story forms as occasions for survivance, in contrast to ethnographic or social science essays, which take up the opportunity for cultural surveillance and dominance and in which the "*indian*, the simulation of the scapegoat, has no referent more than sacrifice and violence" (31). Literality and orality in "Wistful Envies" leads Vizenor to consider the writings, especially the autobiographical writings, of "varionatives" such as Jamake Highwater who fabricate for themselves an "*indian*" identity. The concept of "transmotion" is explored in a number of essays: "Literary Animals," "Native Transmotion," and "Fugitive Poses." Transmotion is a visionary practice and characteristic of native storiers; it names ontological movement or transformation as well as geographical moves. The imaginative freedom of transmotion expresses the presence of tribal sovereignty and, in this way, survivance. In stories, pictomyths, "native virtual cartography" (173), the separation of animal and human (which in Anglo-American culture is the domination of natives and nature) is reversed by ontological transformation or tribal transmotion. More than this, native movement is an assertion of presence that is neither granted nor controlled by government: "Motion is a natural human right that is not bound by borders" (188–89). Tribal movement, then, is an assertion of political sovereignty independent of the provisions of colonialist treaties. Treaties regulate sovereignty over land but not over people, and transmotion is an assertion of this sovereignty of the people. The book concludes with a call to "we the people": "We, the natives of this continent, are the storiers of presence, and we actuate the observance of natural reason and transmotion in this constitutional democracy" (199).

CHAPTER 3

Gerald Vizenor as Poet

Vizenor's first published works were collections of poetry—volumes of haiku inspired by the time he spent in Japan and consolidated by his academic work in Asian studies. Many of these early books were published by Nodin Press, which Vizenor established in Minneapolis in 1967 and sold soon after and which continues to publish books by local writers and on topics of relevance to Minnesota. His first volume was *Two Wings the Butterfly* (1962), followed by *Raising the Moon Vines* (1964, 1968), *Slight Abrasions: A Dialogue in Haiku* with Jerome Downes (1966), *Empty Swings* (1967), and *Seventeen Chirps* (1964, 1968); Vizenor has continued to return to this poetic genre, as evidenced by the publication of *Matsushima: Pine Islands* (1984), *Water Striders* (1989), and *Cranes Arise: Haiku Scenes* (1999). A volume of longer poems, *Almost Ashore*, appeared in 2006, and the epic narrative poem *Bear Island: The War at Sugar Point* was published in the same year. The latter section of this chapter is devoted to a discussion of the important "epic haiku" that is *Bear Island*. First, the poetic contexts and tradition within which Vizenor's poetry are situated need to be clarified. Vizenor's retellings of Frances Densmore's translation of traditional tribal songs in volumes such as *Anishinabe nagamon: Songs of the People* and *Summer in the Spring: Anishinaabe Lyric Poems and Stories*, introduced in the previous chapter, offer an important poetic source. A concept that recurs in Vizenor's accounts of his work as a poet is "dreamscape," the tribal consciousness into which good poetry leads the reader. At the same time, Vizenor's poetry, like the tribal tradition upon which he draws, is located very specifically in time and place. This specificity raises the issue of language and the capacity of language to capture the moment in a particular locale.

In a 1981 interview with Neal Bowers and Charles Silet, Vizenor responds to the question of how he experiences writing in English. "English is not a good language into which tribal, oral expressions can be translated," he observes. "That doesn't mean there's anything wrong with English; it's just a different language, a language of commerce and technology, a language without much place, without much spirit of place. Tribal languages are concrete, a symbolic connection to place. Tribal languages were spoken in places for thousands and thousands of years, and for that reason the place words are more dramatic connections to the earth. In tribal language and religion there are connections between vision, word, and place. And where people have visions, the vision was connected to the energies of the earth through words, a complex abstract connection. The word has power in its context, in its sentences, in the structure of the paragraph, in mythic and linear networks, but it's difficult to find power in words of place in translation."[1] Vizenor emphasizes that translation of the oral tradition is neither his aim nor his interest; rather, he is engaged in reimagining and reexpressing the tribal oral tradition, by recreating that connection between vision, word, and place. This he achieves in his visionary poetic style, which brings together the most effective aspects of Japanese haiku and Anishinaabe dream songs in a Western literary context that some scholars have likened to European modernist or imagist poetry.[2]

In her study of Vizenor's work, *Gerald Vizenor: Writing in the Oral Tradition*, Kimberly Blaeser offers a compact definition of haiku:

The haiku is a short poem (generally classified as a lyric) usually made up of seventeen syllables in three lines, which follow a 5-7-5 syllable pattern. Although English and Japanese haiku may differ in regard to the use of poetic techniques such as rhyme and alliteration, both rely mainly on cadence, not meter, for their rhythm. The poem most frequently has as its subject some aspect or observation of nature and usually includes a seasonal element. Tightly constructed, it offers vivid images with little or no commentary or interpretation. . . . The haiku celebrates the "suchness" of things themselves and frequently has its origin in an experience of personal enlightenment.[3]

Haiku is an intensely disciplined and constrained, concise poetic form. Theme, syllabic structure, line length, cadence, and style of imagery all are highly prescribed by the haiku tradition. Tom Lynch has wondered at the possible attraction of haiku for a tribal writer, and he argues that, in fact, the relevance of this stylized Japanese form to a writer working in a tribal context lies in the tension that haiku generates between the eternal and a precise observed moment. "This juxtaposition of permanence and change," Lynch writes, "might also suggest a parallel to the condition of the postindian tribes confronting the dilemma of how to maintain tribal being yet remain alive to the flux of the contemporary world, not a 'fossilized generalization' in a colonialist matrix."[4] Haiku, then, offers a way of expressing simultaneously a sense of tribal heritage and contemporary change, of a fixed past and an ephemeral present. For example, one of Vizenor's early haiku, the poem that opens *Raising the Moon Vines*, reads:

old windmill
locked with rust over the well
takes on the wind[5]

In this poem four nouns are brought into imagistic play: wind-mill, rust, well, and wind. The image "locked with rust" in con-junction with the adjective "old" suggests a fixed and unchanging temporal condition. However, the image of the wind is conven-tionally associated with change, often violent change. The chal-lenge of the static windmill that "takes on" the wind can then be interpreted as a challenge of the past to present change. There is a distinctly modern and midwestern tone to the poem about a rusted windmill. Rather more tribal in tone is this haiku from the later collection, *Cranes Arise:*

> *grand marais, minnesota*
> timber wolves
> raise their voices overnight
> trickster stories[6]

In this poem there are two voices juxtaposed: the howling of the wolves and the stories of the tribal trickster. The structure of the poem suggests that the wolves' voices are telling "trickster stories" but these voices are heard only "overnight," temporar-ily and on a particular occasion. In contrast the trickster stories begin with the origin myth of the tribe; the trickster is a perma-nent agent in tribal mythology. In this poem, rather than the fixed being challenged by change (like the rusted windmill), the ephemeral finds an echo in the stability of the tribal past.

In the two haiku discussed above, the shape of the poem on the page broadly conforms to the line structure prescribed for classic haiku. As Blaeser describes, haiku consist of three lines arranged in a "5-7-5 syllable pattern." While the precise number of syllables may not be observed, the longer central line enclosed by shorter lines describes the structure Vizenor creates for all his haiku poetry. Also in conformity with the classic haiku form, the poems address an aspect of nature, related to the seasons, in a sequence of vivid images that carry no authorial comment or interpretation. Both books of haiku are organized into four seasonally themed sections: *Cranes Arise* begins with a section of autumn poems and *Raising the Moon Vines* with spring poems. In the technical detail of his haiku poems, Vizenor respects the Japanese poetic tradition. However, in an interview with Jack Foley, Vizenor agrees that haiku brought him to a new appreciation of his own tribal literature "by way of imagery."[7] In the 1981 conversation with Bowers and Silet, Vizenor comments upon but does not attempt a definitive statement about the relationship between tribal and Japanese poetic forms, or what he calls "the mythic parallel between haiku and dream songs." He continues: "It didn't occur to me until after I had studied both forms. It's difficult to tell whether Ojibwe dream songs are like haiku or whether haiku are like dream songs. There are similarities, with the exception of ego in dream songs, which is dominant; in haiku, of course, it's much more subtle. But that intensity of imagery and the idea of comparisons—the kind of mythical transformations, comparisons between human behavior, and comparisons in life without a superior relationship to it—are certainly not unusual in literature, but there is a difference culturally. And that difference shows, I feel, in haiku, and it shows, of course, in tribal dream songs, and in almost all tribal literature, oral literature."[8] The importance of juxtaposition as an imagistic technique that creates powerful but hermeneutically open comparisons links the two styles of expression: haiku and dream songs. This very openness, where the poet does not indicate the thematic nature of the comparison, creates possibilities for what Vizenor here describes as "mythical transformations." This poem from *Cranes Arise*, for example, juxtaposes allusion to the tribal trickster figure with a mundane scarecrow:

clear lake, minnesota
trickster moon
lingers behind a scarecrow
crown prince

Perhaps the moonlight casts a shadow that appears to "crown" the scarecrow, elevating this figure to a higher status; perhaps the transformative effect of the light is to create a trickster of the scarecrow; perhaps the scarecrow is indeed the trickster but this identity is apparent only by moonlight. All of these interpretations are possible. In each the scarecrow and the trickster are somehow mythically transformed. The intensity of the imagery and the power of the comparison between the two figures generates a rich range of potential meanings. It is this capacity of imagistic poetry, as in haiku and dream song, that Vizenor develops in his work.

Kimberly Blaeser also points out the similarity between the two poetic forms: "Both haiku and dream songs are tightly constructed poetic units with vivid images (often of nature) and with little commentary, meant to transport the reader beyond the words to an experience or what Vizenor calls a 'dreamscape.'"[9] The visual nature of poetic imagination and the experience of "dreamscape" is key to understanding Vizenor's poetry, though this quality characterizes his prose writings as well. Both tribal and Japanese poetic traditions emphasize the visual and contribute to this aspect of Vizenor's imagistic poetry. But the origins of these poetic styles in a particular national or tribal culture is of little significance to Vizenor. When asked by A. Robert Lee whether he set out to "Americanize" the Japanese poetic tradition of haiku, in either structure or subject matter, Vizenor replied that "my haiku scenes are the tease of seasons, not cultures or nations. The seasons create the haiku scenes, and the images are common, not exotic."[10] Vizenor goes on to point out the ways in which poetic images can transcend the differences and separations of cultures, nations, and historical times by explaining his sense of connection with past Japanese writers of haiku, such as Yosa Buson, Matsuo Basho, and Kobayashi Issa, which he experiences while reading their work; "we meet by nature in the book," he says.[11]

In his essay "Envoy to Haiku" (1993), Vizenor describes three stages in the development of his career as a writer of haiku. He refers to the poems of the first volumes, such as *Raising the Moon Vines*, as "common comparative experiences in the past tense."[12] The poems included in the later volume, *Matsushima: Pine Islands* (1984), he describes as "more metaphorical, concise, and with a sense of presence." In the third stage of his development as a writer of haiku, he adds an "envoy" or prose gloss to the haiku poem in order to "widen the sentiment and attitude of the poem" into a tribal context.[13] Illustrating this latter point, Vizenor discusses in the essay four examples, which include his very first haiku poem:

> calm in the storm
> master basho soaks his feet
> water striders

To this poem is added the following envoy:

> The striders listen to the wind, the creation of sound that is heard and seen in the motion of water; the wind teases the tension and natural balance on the surface of the world. The same wind that moves the spiders teases the poets.[14]

The figure of "master basho" mentioned in the poem is the historical Japanese master of haiku poetry, Matsuo Basho. "Water striders" are the delicate insects that use the surface tension of water to defy gravity and walk on the surface of water. The physical tension of the water's surface finds a comparison in the tension between calm and stormy weather conditions. Both the poem and the envoy operate on the basis of comparison, but the comparisons are different. In the poem both the insects and the poet place their feet on the water; in the envoy both the insects and the poet are touched by the wind in comparable "teasing" ways. However, the envoy introduces the figure of the wind. This does not appear in the poem. So the envoy is more than a simple interpretation of or commentary about the poem; the envoy is a supplementary aesthetic object that enhances and extends the occasion and the meanings of the haiku.

The envoy adds a layer of interpretive intervention between the poem and the reader and in this way can be said to violate one of the principles of haiku: that the reader must be entirely free to construct the meaning of the poem. Given that he respects the prescribed form of haiku elsewhere in his work, why should Vizenor depart so radically from it with the creation of these envoys? This question is echoed in the questions Kimberly Blaeser asks in her 1997 essay, "'Interior Dancers': Transformations of Vizenor's Poetic Vision": "What links can there be between Vizenor the satirist and political activist, the Vizenor of trickster literature, and Vizenor the haiku master? What connections between the cutting sarcasm of his social criticism and the mystical reaches of his poetic voice?"[15] She gives a brief answer to these questions when she observes that "Vizenor's voice and poetic vision have always reflected the dynamic reality of Anishinaabe experience, both contemporary and historical. His poetry, like his prose, issues at once lament, loud laughter, biting criticism, natural wisdom, and spiritual insight. He is, within his poetry, at once ironist, trickster, word warrior, and tribal dreamer."[16] The relationship between the haiku poem and the prose envoy offers in miniature a model of the relationship between Vizenor's writing in poetry and in prose. Mutually enriching, the combination of distinct literary genres underlines the transformative power of his literary voice. This is present in the early haiku poetry and this quality of his writing is sustained through the changes of genre as he moved increasingly to prose and novel writing.

The collection *Matsushima: Pine Islands* draws together many of the characteristics of Vizenor's haiku poetry.[17] The volume is divided into four sections according to the seasons, "Autumn Haiku," "Winter Haiku," "Spring Haiku," and "Summer Haiku," which are of unequal length. All of Vizenor's collections of haiku are organized according to the season, though the seasons do not appear in the same order in each collection. The importance of seasonal context is emphasized by Vizenor's inclusion of the relevant Japanese calligraphic signs not only on the page that names the section but also, in the case of collections like *Matsushima* and *Cranes Arise*, in the middle of each page, thus separating the two haiku printed on each page.[18] The passing of time as the reader moves through the collection as a whole is indicated by occasional first lines that include mention of a specific month of the year. The eleventh poem of the Autumn sequence begins "October moonrise"; the seventeenth poem begins "warm October wind"; the penultimate poem of the section begins "November storm," thus prefacing the transition to the Winter section, in which no specific months are mentioned. However, the first poem of the Spring section begins "April ice storm," and we are reminded by the opening lines of the fourth poem, "April tolls," and the fifth, "march moon," that we are moving with the poet through the yearly seasonal cycle. The fourteenth of the Summer section begins "August clouds," and the twenty-second poem opens with the image "cold rain in August," locating the sequence in the closing phase of summer. These references to the passage of the seasons, embedded in the opening images of the poems, contribute to the coherence of the poem sequence as a whole. Similarly the poems of *Matsushima* are characterized by verbal echoes and word patterns. To take one example, one poem in the Winter section reads:

> grave birds
> toast the new names in stone
> perched on plastic flowers

This striking image of funeral flowers made of plastic recurs in the Spring section in the poem that reads:

> white butterflies
> flutter over a bridal wreath
> plastic flowers

These images appear again, in close proximity to each other, in the closing pages of the collection. Five poems from the end of the Summer section we read, "white butterflies / wave from the bridal wreath / nuptial ironies." As if to underline the connection between the absent plastic flowers that previously occupied the place of "nuptial ironies" in the third line and death, a link established in the Spring poem, the late Summer poem that follows this reads "cold rain / old friends huddle at a grave / umbrellas waver." The verbal echoes of white butterflies, associated with human rituals such as marriage and funerals and the modern industrial image of plastic flowers, echoes across the seasons and links the various sections of *Matsushima*. A further example of this verbal patterning is the image of the school bell, which in the Spring poem sounds when the children hit it with stones ("April tolls / children stone the school bell / willow buds") but in the Summer poem is sounded by hail stones ("hail stones / sound once or twice a summer / old school bell"). The difference between these poems, the absence of children from school during the summer holiday, marks the difference of the seasons. A dramatic image that recurs throughout *Matsushima* is the barbed-wire fence. In the early Summer poem nature asserts its presence and disguises the aggressive fences: "bold nasturtiums / dress the barbed wire fences / down to the wild sea." The negative connotations of the dangerous barbed wire are emphasized in the late Summer poem, which also stresses the unnatural and manufactured quality of the wire: "plastic animals / leap back from the barbed wire / curtains on the line." Earlier in *Matsushima* the late Spring poem introduces the image of barbed wire in a more benign way: "new settlers / weave their nests with horse hair / carded on the fence." We might assume that "new settlers" must be human, but the second line clarifies that these settlers are birds that visit seasonally. Barbed wire is not mentioned by name, only by function as that which catches the hair of passing horses' tails and helpfully unknots or "cards" the hair, which is then available as building material for the birds' nests. In the case of this image of barbed wire, Vizenor presents different aspects of this object in nature but the recurrence of the image lends coherence and unity to the haiku sequence.

Kimberly Blaeser, in describing the characteristic thematic structure of Vizenor's individual haiku poems, notes that "the working of much of Vizenor's haiku . . . first evokes a sense of time and place, next adds the presence of animal life and a tribal consciousness, and finally, enlivens the scene with spiritual significance."[19] Vizenor confirms this characteristic poetic structure in the introduction to *Cranes Arising* (1999), where he remarks that "the haiku scenes are arranged in the four seasons, a natural connection of imagist poems. The season is suggested in the first line of most haiku poems. . . . The second line of many haiku poems presents the action, the sense of motion, the natural reason and tension of the image . . . . The last line of a haiku poem teases a sense of presence, a sensation, and traces coincidence, consciousness, or contingency" (n.p.). We have seen how Vizenor inflects the opening image with a seasonal reference or the name of the month in which the poem is set. As Blaeser notes, these opening images are often indicative of where the poem is set. In *Matsushima* we find examples that clearly establish the poetic setting, including "broken fence" (twelfth of the Autumn poems), which suggests that the poet is looking at a meadow though in fact the next line clarifies that the setting is an orchard ("horses high in the orchard"); "corner diner" (twelfth of the Winter poems), which establishes an urban setting; "pacific breeze," which creates a seaside setting confirmed by the closing image of "sailboats on the bay" (seventh of the Spring poems); and, among the Summer poems, "ocean sunset" (third poem) and "suburban bees" (fifth poem).[20]

The second or middle lines of Vizenor's haiku poems usually begins with a verb. In this way, as Blaeser comments, he "adds the presence of animal life and a tribal consciousness" or, in Vizenor's own words, in the second line he introduces "the action, the sense of motion, the natural reason and tension of the image." If we return to the poems discussed earlier, we find that "grave birds / toast" and "white butterflies / flutter." Because the second lines begin with a verb, these poems are structured in the syntactical sequence of a standard English sentence: subject-verb-object. Other poems resist this kind of logical structure and instead work exclusively on the principle of imagistic juxtaposition. The second lines of these poems do not begin with the verb; rather, the verb forms part of the image. In the first poem of the Autumn section of *Matsushima*, "calm in the storm / master basho soaks his feet / water striders," the verb occurs in the central position of the central line of the poem. The verb "soaks" is in tension with the closing image of "water striders" because these insects walk on the surface of the water; they do not immerse or "soak" their feet. And yet Vizenor's homage to Master Basho's mastery of the haiku form suggests that the master poet can figuratively be said to walk on water, to defy ordinary human limitations. The juxtaposition of the images—of storm, of soaking feet, of water insects—leaves open the final significance of the many possible comparisons and contrasts among them.

The final line of Vizenor's haiku poems establishes the significance of the preceding two lines but without imposing a final semantic closure upon the poem. This significance varies in kind, as Vizenor explains: The final line "teases a sense of presence, a sensation, and traces coincidence, consciousness, or contingency." So the coincidence of Master Basho's foot bath and the image of the water striders may be a matter of pure contingency, though it may also provide an insight into the poet's consciousness. The convergence of the human and insect worlds is taken up in the following poem in *Matsushima*: "fat green flies / square dance across the grapefruit / honor your partner." The visual likeness of human partners meeting in a barn dance and flies meeting across the cut face of a grapefruit draws out a coincidence that also expresses the presence in the human world of

creatures usually considered insignificant. As Tom Lynch remarks, often Vizenor's haiku focus on the smallest creatures in
the natural world; he does this not in a symbolic way, where
these creatures would reveal meaning that is important in human
terms, but by placing the poet as a witness or observer of their
nonhuman activities.[21] Haiku, such as this poem, focuses upon
kinds of meaning that are located outside human comprehension. The juxtaposition of unrelated images, such as a square
dance and flies, emphasizes paradox and privileges intuition over
intellect. The final line of the haiku poem is intended to dissolve
meaning into enlightenment rather than resolve the poetic lines
into a message or discursive interpretation. "If a Japanese haiku
seems a meaningless image to a Western reader," Lynch explains,
"it is not because that reader lacks familiarity with Japanese culture and so misses the symbolic significance, it is because the
haiku is indeed, perversely, meaningless."[22]

The dissolution of meaning that is part of the haiku form
lends Vizenor's poetry a deconstructive power that he applies to
"terminal creeds." The absolute distinction between human and
nonhuman worlds is one of the destructive beliefs or terminal
creeds that Vizenor addresses. His haiku poems frequently
address the coincidence of animal or insect life with the human
realm. This poem, and this image of square-dancing flies, is cited
by A. Robert Lee as an example of the humor that arises in
Vizenor's haiku as a result of the tension created between nature
and human civilization.[23] In her 1986 appreciation of Vizenor's
writing, "Woodland Word Warrior," A. LaVonne Brown Ruoff
likens Vizenor's "playfulness and wry humor" to that of Robert
Frost. Ruoff takes as her example the poem "Tyranny of
Moths," one of thirteen poems published in *Voices of the Rainbow*, the 1975 anthology edited by Kenneth Rosen. Certainly

the lines she quotes are reminiscent of Frost's famous poem "The Road Not Taken":

> tonight the moths
> go stitching with their kind
> up and down the net
> they may never know
> my light is not my day
>
> . . . .
>
> switching out the light
> we are drawn to another light
> farther down the road.[24]

Vizenor's play on pronouns ("they," "my," and "we") adds a layer of complexity to this encounter between two alien world views. The moths may well believe that the artificial light constitutes the human day, though Vizenor's use of the double negative construction complicates this meaning, but they will not know the always-unfulfilled desire that makes humans yearn for "another light." The shifts from third person ("their kind") to first-person singular ("my day") and then to third-person plural ("we are") take place in a highly imagistic structure that lacks punctuation and so requires that readers provide causal connections between the phrases. For example, it is possible to read these lines as including a significant parenthesis to read "they may never know . . . we are drawn to another road." Alternatively, what the moths do not know and what "we are drawn to" may be completely autonomous entities. Throughout his poetry, Vizenor uses the absence of punctuation to generate indeterminacy and a multiplicity of meanings.

The lack of punctuation and the refusal of uppercase typography (so even proper names appear in lowercase) are characteristics of Vizenor's haiku poetry that also mark his longer poems.

The primary structural principle of these longer poems is described by Tom Lynch as "incremental parallelisms."[25] This stylistic characteristic requires the reader to identify and keep in mind verbal parallels that build and echo throughout the poem. These parallels or echoes are similar to the word patterns that link poems within haiku sequences such as *Matsushima*. Upon the reader then is placed a burden of visual remembrance; the reader must hold in mind the images that recur throughout the poem—plastic flowers or barbed wire, to return to examples given previously. In *Postindian Conversations* Vizenor recalls his first exposure, in Japan, to the powerful visual element of haiku: "Haiku held me to my own visual memories, not to mere tradition, and taught me that creation is in an imagistic scene. Haiku also taught me about ambiguities, and the natural impermanence of life and literature."[26] Here he suggests not only that he learned to write haiku but also that haiku served as a vehicle to teach him about poetry. His choice of theme or subject, for example, would not be a matter of "mere tradition" but would be the "visual memories" that he captures in words. And the meaning of the poem, expressed through the theme, would be the resistance to fixed messages: ambiguity, impermanence, and the dynamic quality of meaning.

These techniques—the use of incremental parallelisms, visual imagery, and the dissolution of meaning—create what Kimberly Blaeser calls "an 'open' text, a text that advertises its absences and requires the response of the reader to bring it to fruition, a text that works to activate the reader's imagination and this to engage the reader in the process of 'unfixing' the text."[27] In the introduction to *Two Wings the Butterfly*, Vizenor draws attention to the fact that what is valued "in a Japanese ink painting . . . is not the complexity of the detail but the importance of what

is not there."[28] The significance that may be attached to semantic absence is repeated in a number of statements that Vizenor
has made about the nature of his poetry. In "Envoy to Haiku,"
for example, Vizenor discusses what he calls "haiku hermeneutics." He quotes from Roland Barthes's *Empire of Signs*: "The
haiku reminds us of what has never happened to us; in it we
recognize a repetition without origin, an event without cause, a
memory without person, a language without moorings. . . . Here
meaning is only a flash, a slash of light."[29] The poems that are
written to reproduce these effects work on the basis of connotation rather than denotation to evoke rather than describe an
object or experience. This is where juxtaposition is such an important poetic technique, one which characterizes both Vizenor's
earlier and later poetry. The collection *Almost Ashore* (2006) is
divided into three sections, beginning with "Crane Dancers,"
ending with "Natural Duty," and including the middle section
"Haiku Scenes." The poems of this middle section comprise
three verses, each of which is structured as a haiku. Indeed, several verses are previously published haiku presented here in a
new context. The poem "Natural Balance," for example, exemplifies Vizenor's use of imagistic juxtaposition to make present
through absence a paradoxical set of meanings. The middle verse
reads, "gray morning / only a spring daffodil / hides the winter."[30] The setting of the poem, established in the first line, is
"march snow." Consequently the image of a lone daffodil that is
capable of hiding the winter season is paradoxical. The image
makes sense only if we read it as focusing all the poet's attention
away from the pervasive snowy scene. Thus the floral emblem of
impending spring renders winter absent. However, if the reader
insists too strongly on a rational or causal meaning then the
poem's images dissolve into non-sense.

In the introduction to *Matsushima: Pine Islands* (a passage that he also quotes in his 1999 edition of *Raising the Moon Vines*), Vizenor explains this process of semantic dissolution: "Deconstruct the printed words in a haiku and there is nothing; nothing is in a haiku, not even a poem" (n.p.). He continues, in *Matsushima*, to clarify the nature of this absence of poetic meaning. He writes, "The *nothing* in a haiku is not an aesthetic void; rather, it is a moment of enlightenment, a dreamscape where the words dissolve; no critical marks, no grammatical stains remain" (n.p.). The poem, then, is an experience rather than an object for the reader to consume, extracting in the process some kind of meaning or "message." Rather, the poem is something that the reader does by entering the intuitive mode of knowledge invoked by the poet and by opening the imagination to all possible constructions of significance. In such a poem the reader becomes the active agent of meaning by engaging with the poet's mode of "visual thinking," what Vizenor terms, in the introduction to *Matsushima*, "word cinema" (n.p.). This visual quality of imagination, linking poet and reader through the poem, is a further characteristic shared by tribal dream songs and Japanese haiku: in *The Everlasting Sky* Vizenor claims the "*oshki anishinabe* writer is a visual thinker."[31]

In his longer poems the reader is placed in the same creative position. The poems collected in *Almost Ashore* include some of Vizenor's earliest anthologized work, revised and substantially rewritten for this volume. For example, "White Earth" was originally subtitled "Images and Agonies" when an early version appeared in *Voices of the Rainbow*. In the same anthology a version of "Guthrie Theater" was published as "Indians at the Guthrie" together with a version of "Family Photograph," which also appeared in Vizenor's autobiographical *Interior*

Landscapes.[32] These poems use highly visual images that are presented on a single short line and often consist of an adjective or verb followed by a noun. For example, in the relatively long poem "White Earth" we encounter lines such as "October sunrise" (10) or "muted roses" (11), "bright moon / breaks on the bridge" (12) or "mighty ravens / inspire nicknames" (13). Vizenor plays on the positioning of verbs at the beginning of the line with images like "trade pelts" (12), which can be read as a single noun or can be read alternatively in the context of the preceding line ("beaver and muskrat") to mean that pelts are what beaver and muskrats trade ("beaver and muskrat / trade pelts"). The absence of punctuation eases this play on the potential meaning of words and phrases. The emphasis upon single images is then complicated by the use of verbal parallelisms: the tribal woodland is placed in a sustained contrast with federal "civilization," the White Earth Reservation with "the city"; shamans are contrasted with Christian priests, medicine bundles with benedictory beads. Particular images recur in different contexts: the white of White Earth and white pine; the black of "black beads," "black bears," "black lace," and black ravens; and the shadows of native tricksters and the "shadows on a bus" juxtaposed with the flickering shadows of the movies.

A poem such as "White Earth" demonstrates Vizenor's masterly use of figurative language and specifically of metaphor. Elaine Jahner has described how in Vizenor's use of metaphor "one term is founded in the known and proven, the other in the possible and as-yet unknown—grasped only through our intuitive sense of the potential meaning of what we perceive visually."[33] So Vizenor's linguistic comparisons take us from the familiar to the strange, as in the following sequence of images from "White Earth":

> white earth
> shadows on a bus
> last forever
> in late movies (12).

We may be familiar with White Earth as the name of Vizenor's tribal community; we may also be familiar with images of tribal people projected in movies, images that last forever as stereotypes though the film projection of them lasts only a matter of minutes. The bus that takes tribal people from their homes to "the lonesome city" (12, the line preceding those quoted above) may also be familiar. What is strange is the image of "shadows" on the bus. We can perhaps visualize the spectral presence of tribal people leaving their traditional lands, but the image with which Vizenor presents us is of shadows, the absence of people, and the trace of their physical existence. Jahner explains this paradoxical relationship between imagistic presence and absence: "Metaphors are 'visual dream flights,' with a clearly marked starting point and the requirement that their conclusions lead to beneficial connections which, in turn, reveal the incompleteness that leads to other flights, or, to change to another of Vizenor's fundamental images, to further earthdiving. Always though, earthdiving should bring up out of the sea of arbitrariness the stuff with which to build the turtle island, a real, if always incomplete, ground for meaning."[34] Vizenor's use of metaphor, then, is a quest for meaning that places the reader in a parallel position as a fellow searcher for meaning and enlightenment.

This enlightenment is frequently tragic, as Vizenor uncovers the historical experience of the Anishinaabe people under U.S. colonialism. In "White Earth" he offers a sustained metaphorical comparison between Christian missionaries and tribal shamans; in "Family Photograph," as Kimberly Blaeser has shown, he links tribal people and their timber resources through the figure of his murdered father: "my father / clement vizenor / was a spruce / among the trees" (6). Like many tribal people, during the so-called termination period, his father moved from the reservation to the city, and in his poem Vizenor relates this move through a series of images that draw together the government's harvesting of tribal timber and the removal of tribal people:

> corded for pulp
> by federal
> indian agents
> my father
> turned away
> from white earth
> the reservation
> colonial genealogies
> and moved to the city
> with family
> at twenty-three (6)

The lines retain a key ambiguity in terms of what is "corded for pulp": the trees that are not explicitly mentioned or the figure of "my father." As Blaeser argues, "Here Vizenor recognizes in the fate of the timber resources and the Anishinaabe people the same 'clear-cutting' by greedy colonial interests."[35] However, this exploration and exposure of a tragic history never becomes victimry; rather, Vizenor's use of figurative language emphasizes survivance. For example, the poem "Family Photograph" concludes with a series of images that place his father's death and the rapacious theft of tribal resources within the context of Anishinaabe myth and storytelling. His father, the metaphorical figure that links one particular tribal person with the historical events of the entire tribe, at the end of the poem is said to have "moved to the city / and lost at cards" (9). Thus it is the evil Gambler of Anishinaabe myth who explains the evil explored in the events of the poem. This is not to represent these events as any less evil but to place them in a context where these experiences are owned by the tribal poet and his family, where the discourses of imposed "victimry" can be resisted.

Vizenor's most ambitious poetic project to date is the epic historical poem *Bear Island: The War at Sugar Point* (2006), which consists of a prose introduction followed by six sections in verse: "Overture: Manidoo Creations," "Bagwana: The Pillagers at Liberty," "Hole in the Day: Grafters and Warrants," "Bearwalkers: 5 October 1898," "Gatling Gun: 6 October 1898," and "War Necklace: 9 October 1898." The poem recounts the circumstances and events of the little-known last of the "Indian Wars": the battle between the Pillagers of the Leech Lake Reservation and the U.S. Third Infantry Regiment, which, though heavily outnumbered, the tribal warriors won. In an interview with John Purdy and Blake Hausman, Vizenor gives an account of how *Bear Island* came into being. He tells how originally he had intended to write a historical essay and spent five years researching this incident. He even hired an assistant to exhaust all possible sources of documentary information, but finally he concluded that the story could not be told adequately without the creative filling in of gaps in the documentary record. Consequently Vizenor turned to the idea of writing a long narrative poem, but he was dissatisfied with the result, which, as he describes it, was flawed by "too many connections, causative statements, prepositional phrases. It just ended up junky and kind of ponderous and phony."[36] The poem he finally published took the form, again in his words, of "one fifty-page haiku imagistic poem about this battle."[37] So that readers would understand the neglected historical context of the poem, he then wrote an extensive prose narrative to introduce the work.

Bear Island is a comic mock-epic imagistic poem that recollects the hostile military engagement in 1898 between the Anishinaabe Pillagers and the U.S. Army, a story that subverts the dominant narrative of U.S. history by telling of native triumph and in this way serves the interests of tribal survivance. As Jace Weaver points out in his foreword to the poem, the defeat of the Third Infantry at Bear Island took place three years after the historian Frederick Jackson Turner declared the frontier closed[38] and eight years after the Wounded Knee Massacre of 1890. The poetic style is lyrical, with clear influences from Vizenor's practice of haiku and tribal dream songs. *Bear Island* is an inspired performance that uses figurative language to straddle the rhetorical distinction between individual and communal, past and present, comic and tragic modes of experience. In this poem Vizenor creates a history of United States–native relations that is based on tribal agency rather than the false stories of victimry promoted in official histories. *Bear Island*, then, is an exercise in what Vizenor calls native *sovenance*, "that sense of presence in remembrance, that trace of creation and natural reason in native stories; . . . the connotation of sovenance is a native presence . . . not that romance of an aesthetic absence or victimry."[39] In this poem Vizenor answers the many tellings of the genocidal atrocities to which tribal people were subject: the Wounded Knee Massacre, the Sand Creek Massacre, and the Mystic River Massacre (events that play an important role in poems like "Guthrie Theater" in *Almost Ashore*). *Bear Island* is a survivance poem in which victimry is refused, a massacre is averted, and tribal warriors are triumphant. Native survivance, in this epic poem, is opposed both to native victimry and U.S. triumphalism.

The poem begins with the "Overture: Manidoo Creations," which establishes, as the primary interpretive context, Anishinaabe creation stories. At the same time this "overture" introduces an ongoing history of genocide through Vizenor's citation of the Sand Creek Massacre, the events at the Little Big Horn, the Allotment Act, the outbreak of smallpox on the Plains—in short, the history in which interpretation of the Bear Island uprising must be located. Throughout the poem holds in balance three interrelated threads: the events leading to and constituting the specific conflict, which are told in a lyric or elegiac mode; the history of U.S. genocide against native people, which is narrated in an ironic mock-epic mode that subverts the grand rhetoric of westward expansionism; and the imagistic thread of tribal consciousness, which is told in visual totemic images. This threefold structure works to bring the reader beyond the restrictions of linear narrative and into the realm of the tribal imagination and shamanic vision. Unifying the various sections of the poem are patterns of repeated images, such as we have seen in Vizenor's shorter poems. In *Bear Island* animal images such as the totemic bear, otters, wolves, and beavers; tree images such as cedar boughs, silver birch, white pine, and sumacs; and bird images such as ravens, cranes, and cedar waxwings recur in a pattern of echoes and allusions that makes present a symbolic subtext that enhances and complicates Vizenor's more explicit narrative storytelling. This balanced tripartite structure also serves to tell a tragic story—a terrible last installment in the bloody history of the United States' westward expansion—but to tell this story as a native triumph of intelligence, stealth, and courage.

The story begins in September 1898 with the refusal of the Anishinaabe warrior and leader of the Pillager band, Bugonay-geshig ("Hole in the Day"), and another man to testify against a liquor trader at the Onigum Agency on the Leech Lake Reservation. When they were compelled by a federal deputy marshall to depart for the court in Duluth, a party of tribal warriors helped them escape, resulting in warrants for the arrest of the two fugitives and those who had assisted their escape. The Third Infantry, seventy-seven enlisted men under the command of two officers, was summoned and arrived on October 5, 1898, at Sugar Point, where they occupied Bugonaygeshig's cabin and vegetable garden. The shooting started when a rifle accidentally discharged. Maj. Melville Cary Wilkinson took three bullets, five enlisted men were killed and eleven wounded, and there were no reports of native casualties. The newspaper reports that appeared soon after this military encounter referred to "the battle of Leech Lake." A few days later, on October 10, 1898, the U.S. commissioner of Indian Affairs arrived in Minnesota to meet with the Pillagers at Bear Island. As a result of that meeting, the warriors who had helped Bugonaygeshig escape the custody of the federal deputy were arrested. On October 21 all the Pillager warriors were found guilty and received sentences that varied from monetary fines to prison terms. However, on December 13 the Indian Office recommended that the fines be remitted and the prison terms commuted; pardons followed on June 3, 1899. As Vizenor remarks in his introduction to the poem, this was a U.S. defeat "seldom mentioned in military histories" (10).

"Bagwana: The Pillagers at Liberty" begins by invoking the invasion of tribal lands by European immigrants, as "native rights" are contrasted with "constitutional / greed and guile" and the first stanza concludes with the dominance of "treaty decadence / over native liberty" (19). This section establishes the tribal precedence and custom within the context of which Bugonaygeshig acts when he resists the federal U.S. legal system. In this section Vizenor introduces the figure of Bagwana (By My Heart), who achieved fame by tracking a band of Dakota warriors who had killed a Pillager child. This group of fifteen Anishinaabeg threw stones when they had used all their ammunition, and Bagwana, the only survivor, returned to Bear Island a shaman. Bagwana provides the tribal model for Bugonaygeshig's actions one hundred years later, no longer against the Dakota but now against the new enemy, the Americans. The litany of injustices, genocidal violence, and outright frauds committed against tribal communities by this new enemy is supplemented in the following section, "Hole in the Day: Grafters and Warrants," with the specific crimes committed against the Anishinaabe Pillagers in the lead up to the conflict at Sugar Point. Hungry children and cold shivering adults await the late arrival of the treaty-guaranteed annuities, out of which they will be cheated by "shady agents" and "federal legacies" (39). It is in this section that Vizenor introduces the seizure of Bugonaygeshig and his rescue by a group of warriors, emphasizing that the federal authorities overreacted to this event and summoned the army to help deal with a supposed native uprising. The following section, "Bearwalkers 5 October 1898," offers portraits of Major Wilkinson and Gen. John Bacon and their journey to Bear Island. The sequence ends with a brief summary that juxtaposes two views of the conflict:

> nineteen natives
> bear island pillagers

> defeated eighty
> third infantry
> officers and soldiers
> blue immigrants
> mean citizens
> newspaper reporters
> cornered that autumn
> in a bloody garden
> hole in the day
> by my heart
> trace of native shamans
> soared overhead
> with the ravens
> in the white pine
> and mighty maples (72–73)

The stanza begins with an objective account and moves via the poet's pejorative adjectives ("blue immigrants / mean citizens") to the tribal presence of Bugonaygeshig and Bagwana ("hole in the day / by my heart") in the native scene of the conflict.

The two concluding sections turn to the aftermath of the conflict. "Gatling Gun: 6 October 1898" opens with the arrival, as reinforcements, of Lt. Col. Abram Horbach, two hundred soldiers, and a Gatling gun. They arrive in time to deal with the dead and wounded, "never to fight / hole in the day / bear island pillagers" because, as the following lines indicate, "the chance war / closed overnight" (77). In Bugonaygeshig's garden they find, amid the cabbages, "bloody blue wool / dusted with snow" (78) and the haunting sounds of native rattles. The dead man was Pvt. Daniel Schallenstocker, who was driven by hunger to dig for potatoes in Bugonaygeshig's garden; he was shot by a young Pillager warrior who fired "to forewarn / the military poachers" (80). This image of the hungry soldier and the native warrior protecting his land and livelihood captures the compassion Vizenor expresses for both sides in this conflict. The "immigrant" soldiers who simply follow orders are also sacrificed to this war, which was "provoked by arrogance / federal agents / greedy grafters / mercenaries of the white pine" (81). The final section is titled "War Necklace: 9 October 1898," an image that Vizenor remembered from a photograph. In the essay "Imagic Presence: Native Pictomyths and Photographs" (2006), Vizenor notes that "Bugonaygeshig, or bagine giizhig, Hole in the Day, an eminent native warrior, was photographed by James S. Drysdale, Walker, Minnesota, shortly after the war at Sugar Point, near Bear Island in Leech Lake."[40] In that photograph, as Vizenor describes it, Hole in the Day is depicted wearing a fedora and ammunition belt and holds a Winchester rifle. Most interesting to Vizenor, however, is the heavy necklace that Hole in the Day wears, "a collection of spent rifle shells fired by the army at Sugar Point. The necklace is an ironic remembrance of native survivance."[41] In the poem these shells are collected from among "bloody potatoes / and wounded cabbages" (86), the bathos of the image reflecting the farcical nature of the conflict. And yet men died, and Vizenor with characteristic compassion devotes a stanza in remembrance of each of the dead or wounded infantrymen. Though what is noted of men like the military doctor, Herbert Harris, is that he stole a sacred birchbark scroll, an iconic theft that represents metonymically the theft of land, treaty rights, and native liberty by the "wicked agents / timber barons" through "cultural conceits / and constitutional trickery" (93).

In *Bear Island: The War at Sugar Point* Vizenor brings together themes and poetic techniques from his earlier work in a masterly epic portrait of colonial evil and native survivance. He celebrates the Pillager victory over the U.S. Third Infantry but mourns the deaths of those who fell casualty to the violence of American westward expansion. Above all he writes an Anishi-naabe poetic epic, combining thematic references to tribal myths, totems, the midewiwin, and tribal histories with the method of imagistic dream song construction, taking his unique poetic style out of the haiku and into the epic genre.

CHAPTER FOUR

Gerald Vizenor as Dramatist

Vizenor is the author of two dramatic works, the screenplay for the film *Harold of Orange* and the play *Ishi and the Wood Ducks*. Both dramas are characterized by a discursive rather than action structure; that is to say, there is rather more talking than doing in both. Vizenor's drama is lyrical and imagistic in style, like his poetry and fiction. As in his work in other literary genres, Vizenor's drama is marked by a witty and satirical play of language, which is complemented by his use of visual imagery. Indeed, in the genre of drama Vizenor is offered the chance to explore the physical, spatial dimension of narratives, which are performed and actualized before their audiences. Written texts cannot offer this potential to make present the actors in the dramatic narrative. However, in the drama, as in his prose and fictional writings, the issue of narrative perspective or focalization again arises. Vizenor has discussed this as a problem of pronouns: how to involve readers in the text by encouraging them to participate in the "I" viewpoint without falsifying that sense of authorial presence. This issue is affected by the different dramatic forms of film and stage production. A screenplay is written with a view to the camera, which becomes the primary narrative vehicle; in contrast a play is acted on the stage and is thus more immediate, and yet the question of which character's perspective will be brought to the fore is still at issue. And of course in both kinds of drama the choice of actors has a profound impact on how the meanings of the written text (screenplay or play script) will be interpreted. This is particularly important in drama styled like Vizenor's, in which dialogue and verbal exchange dominate.

Harold of Orange: A Screenplay (1984)

The central idea of the screenplay is Harold Sinseer's request for foundation financing for his proposal to establish coffee houses on the reservation. This concept was first published by Vizenor in his 1983 story "Reservation Café: The Origin of American Indian Instant Coffee," which appeared in Simon Ortiz's landmark anthology of Native American short fiction, *Earth Power Coming.*[1] The precise chronological relationship between this story and the screenplay is unclear; in 1983 Vizenor's screenplay was filmed, and in 1984 the film was released. It won Best Film at the San Francisco Film Festival for American Indian Films. Robert Silberman, in his 1985 essay "Gerald Vizenor and *Harold of Orange:* From Word Cinemas to Real Cinema," explains how the screenplay moved to the screen:

> In the spring of 1983 it was announced that a screenplay written by Vizenor had won a competition sponsored by Film in the Cities, a regional media arts center in the Twin Cities of Minnesota. After casting and preliminary work, some of it at Robert Redford's Sundance Institute, the film [directed by Richard Weise] was shot during the summer in and around Minneapolis and St. Paul. Post-production work was done over the winter, and on May 17, 1984, the 30-minute result, *Harold of Orange*, premiered in Minneapolis.[2]

Silberman points out that, despite the creative contribution of the director, actors, and technical crew, the film remains Vizenor's creation. "This is because his collaborators were so determined that the screenplay be respected," Silberman explains. "The original manuscript submitted for the contest went through relatively few changes in the process of being transformed into the shooting script, which in turn was changed in even fewer ways, mostly because of the compromises that are all but inevitable in filmmaking, especially when working on a tight shooting schedule and a low budget."[3] Consequently the film is securely part of Vizenor's oeuvre, and this is underlined by the themes that are shared across Vizenor's writing: the invented nature of the identity category "Indian," the destructive impact of the social sciences and especially anthropology upon tribal cultures and inheritance, the experience of native people in an urban environment, and the role of the trickster in exposing the falsity of "Indian" stereotypes and pointing a productive way forward for tribal communities. As Harold tells the camera in the penultimate shot, "Remember, you were here with some of the best trickster founders of this new earth."[4] The closing shot shows Harold and "the warriors" laughing wildly as the scene fades.[5]

The first publication of the screenplay was in the Fall 1993 issue of the journal *Studies in American Indian Literatures*. Unlike the text reprinted the following year in *Shadow Distance: A Gerald Vizenor Reader* (1994), the 1993 text includes full cast credits, the lyrics to Buffy Sainte-Marie's song, which accompanies the opening and closing credits, and this prefatory text:

> Introduction to the Film
> Harold and the Warriors of Orange
> are descendants of the great trickster
> who created the new earth after the flood.
>
> But the trickster was soon word-driven
> from the land by the white man,

who claimed the earth as his own
and returned to the trickster
only what he couldn't use.

Now, Harold and the Warriors of Orange,
tribal tricksters determined to reclaim
their estate from the white man,
are challenging his very foundations.[6]

In this "Introduction" Vizenor establishes his native characters not simply as trickster figures but also as "earthdivers." In Anishinaabe myth the trickster is trapped in a flood and asks a series of small creatures to dive under the water to find earth; from the few grains of soil retrieved by the muskrat and dried by the trickster Naanabozho, a new earth was created. This story recurs throughout Vizenor's writing, as does the figure of the "new earthdiver," the individual who is able to remake reality from the devastated remains of the old world. In this "Introduction" the old world is the land and culture from which tribal people have been exiled or "word-driven" by the letter of the colonialist law that has deprived them of their traditional territory, by the ideology of manifest destiny, and by the stereotypes of "Indians" that have deprived them of their dignity and autonomy. However, the film promises to show a group of "postindian earthdivers" reclaiming their heritage and building a new world by challenging the dominant white culture. Vizenor plays on the word "foundation": Harold will challenge the discursive foundations of the ideology that has "word-driven" tribal people on to reservations, but he will do this by tricking money from a charitable foundation—not stealing, of course, because Harold is determined to "reclaim [his] estate" and take back some of what has been taken from him as a contemporary native person.

The urban environment in which the action takes place leads Kimberly Blaeser to describe this drama as "postindian," offering "a revealing account of these new places of contact as it tracks the intersections of culture to an urban center and depicts the act of balance and survival undertaken by the tribal characters, [quoting the screenplay] 'trickster founders of this new earth.'"[7]

The structure of the film possesses the classical unity of a single day, as the opening scene is set at sunrise and the closing scene at sunset. The events are framed by these opening and closing scenes that take place in the Harold of Orange Coffee House. At the center of the dramatic structure are three "presentation" scenes in which Harold pitches his proposal to the board of the Bily Foundation; these three scenes are bracketed by scenes set in the board room. Harold persuades the board to agree to an unorthodox method of presenting his proposal, visiting a number of locations around the city. He invites them to a postindian "naming ceremony," which takes place at a fry-bread cart in a parking lot. They visit the artifact cases of the Department of Anthropology then play a baseball game before returning to the board room for the conclusion of Harold's proposal. This peripatetic manner of his presentation offers a number of opportunities for Harold and his colleagues to tease the assumptions about native people held by the board members.

The screenplay is profoundly ironic; indeed, the film itself was financed with foundation money (the Minnesota Screen Project and the Film in the Cities program).[8] From the outset viewers are aware of a number of dramatic ironies. We witness the scene in which Harold discusses with the Warriors of Orange the success of his earlier proposal to grow miniature oranges that in fact were sourced from an organic farmer and passed off to the foundation directors as tribally-produced fruit. Harold's new proposal, for coffee houses on the reservation, will be similarly tricky. As viewers, however, we have a similarly ironic relationship with the foundation board. In the scene that takes place before Harold and the Warriors arrive, we hear the foundation's director, Kingsley Newton, tell his colleagues that Harold's proposal has already been accepted but that Harold has not been informed and they will indulge their desire to hear his "unusual" proposal presented in the "oral tradition."[9] We also learn through her silent recollection that another member of the board, Fannie Mason, had an affair with Harold some years earlier that ended when Harold borrowed money from her for what he described as his tribal grandmother's funeral. When Fannie and Harold finally meet in scene 4, she takes up this issue of her money and his grandmother. "She died four times that year, right?" (307), Fannie demands of Harold. When he defends himself with the argument that such strategies allowed him to survive, she retorts that he survived "on fake funerals and borrowed money" (308).

In the opening scenes, then, Vizenor places the viewer in a privileged position, where the secrets of the various characters, though hidden from each other, are apparent to the viewer. The theme of secrets is particularly important here. Each group of characters protects their secrets and the actions this leads them to take shape the dramatic action. Fannie demands the return of her one thousand dollars in exchange for her support of Harold's coffee house proposal—but viewers know that she knows the proposal has been approved so her support is irrelevant; Harold knows that the proposal itself is a performance with little relevance to the true transaction taking place. He tells Fannie, "You know the old foundation game, we get the money and the foundation gets the good name" (308). Whether Harold's oranges are produced on the reservation or by an organic farmer in the Southwest is irrelevant to the rules of this particular game. That this is understood by both sides in the "game" is emphasized when a member of the foundation board remarks to Harold, "Pinch beans will give us all a good name" (328). Like the best satire, *Harold of Orange* does not offer us a single standard of truth and morality against which the characters can be judged; all of the characters are compromised in some way.

This is especially true of the main character, Harold the trickster. In an interview with Jack Foley, Vizenor describes Harold as a "compassionate trickster" who "did better than people would have expected of him."[10] Laura Coltelli, in the course of interviewing Vizenor, asks why, in this drama, "the trickster is more of a businessman or entrepreneur, a new capitalist," to which Vizenor responds that his trickster characters have always been successful at something (in Harold's case entrepreneurship), but, more important, his tricksters are characterized by "a kind of unmotivated and unrewarding compassion."[11] This is significant, Vizenor explains, because the trickster is also "a very tricky and manipulative person" who easily could be mistaken for a con man or fraudster.[12] This is true of the character of Harold, who is seen in the film taking one thousand dollars from Kingsley (who lends the money so Harold can bury his tribal grandmother) in order to give the money to Fannie.

Here we can appreciate the irony of his name. Harold Sinseer both is and is not the moral standard against which the audience is to measure Vizenor's satire. To the film viewer Harold's name sounds like "sincere." To underline this point, in scene 8 a university police officer mistakes the spelling of his name (321). Yet his sincerity is compromised by his masterful capacity for manipulation (for example, the many times he claims that his tribal grandmother has died). Nonetheless he is a "sin-seer" someone who sees clearly the "sins" or foibles of others. Harold represents himself as a kind of Robin Hood figure, stealing from the rich to give to the poor. He insists to Fannie that he does not steal from people: "The Warriors of Orange are not victims to please the white man. . . . We never cheat people, we are not corrupt politicians with medicine bundles stuffed with false promises. . . . We are imaginative survivors" (308–9). As Karl Kroeber remarks in his introduction to the 1985 special issue of *Studies in American Indian Literatures* devoted to Vizenor's work, "Harold borrows money on the pretext of paying the expenses of his grandmother's funeral in order to repay an earlier loan, obtained on the pretext of paying the expenses of his grandmother's funeral."[13] However, Kroeber quickly qualifies this description of the trickster's playfulness: "But the trickster is also a dark, even a tragic figure. However funny, and he can be very funny, indeed, Vizenor seems to me of contemporary Native American writers the most searching and troubling critic of modern Indians' situation within American culture."[14]

The song performed by Native American singer Buffy Saint-Marie during the opening (and closing) credits raises the issue of the trickster's moral ambivalence, adding to the film version of *Harold of Orange* a dimension of meaning that is not available in the written screenplay. Simply titled "Trickster Song," it is heard in the film as the viewer watches Harold's first appearance on the screen. His transformative power is stressed in the second verse; the third verse plays on the double meaning of the word "lying" to signify both reclining and deceiving:

> Let's reroute some of that money green,
> Move the banks and you move the stream.
> Trickster change how everything seem.
>
> Trickster lying in a bed at night,
> Lying, lying, lying.
> Thinking up schemes to put you right.[15]

The transformative power of dreams and imagination, enacted through the disruptions caused by the trickster, is expressed later in the drama when Kinsley attempts to explain Harold to his colleague Andrew: "He is rather sincere, even innocent, artless at times. . . . He believes that he can stop time and change the world through imagination" (324). Hearing this, Andrew is "nonplussed" until he adds, "With a foundation grant of course" (324), which is confirmed by Kingsley with a knowing smile; "they share the same secret," reads the direction in the screenplay. The trickster can direct some resources from charitable foundations to the reservation community, but at the cost of promoting the charitable reputation of the foundation and its directors.

The song also suggests the paradoxical way in which the trickster works, telling falsehoods in order to get at the truth, creating lying "schemes to put you right." The continual word play, the multiple dramatic ironies of the situation, and the sometimes absurd actions of the trickster and his colleagues have the effect of putting into question the seriousness of Harold and indeed the entire situation.[16] But Vizenor is aware of this. In the "Naming Ceremony" scene, in which Harold and the Warriors use Monopoly cards drawn from a cigar box to select the new names for each of the foundation directors, Kingsley asks Harold, "Are you serious?" to which Harold replies, "Who could be serious about anything in a parking lot at a shopping center . . . use your imagination" (316). The trickster uses absurdity as a way to make a serious point. In the opening scene Harold drives up to the Harold of Orange Coffee House, where hanging in the window is a sign that reads "The New School of Socioacupuncture" (297). For those familiar with Vizenor's neologism "socioacupuncture," it is clear that in the action to follow we will see Harold applying comic pressure to the cultural beliefs and assumptions that perpetuate false images of native people.

The drama is structured so that each scene offers such a comical exposure. James Ruppert remarks that each of the images that focuses the scene is ad hoc and does not develop into a sustained symbolic narrative.[17] However, the episodic structure of the drama works against any sustained use of single image clusters. In scene 1 the primary image is that of the neckties Harold insists all the warriors wear as "uniform" (300) for the presentation. The warrior Son Bear objects that the neckties will turn them all white, that the white man became white because ties constricted the blood circulating to his brain. Harold insists that when the board sees the ties they will hear only "truth" in what they are told. The tribal warriors will seem sufficiently "white" to be believable. This stereotype of Anglo-American culture (the necktie) is balanced against a number of "Indian" stereotypes in the opening scenes. Robert Silberman has noted a visual detail so subtle, as he says, that it almost passes unnoticed: Harold's "orange crates bear labels showing a white businessman with a briefcase: the perfect entrepreneurial emblem for the 1980s, as well as a neat play upon the romanticized images of Indians often used as fruit-crate labels."[18] The romantic attraction of the "Indian" takes on a double significance in the character of Fannie, who is sexually attracted to Harold but who also has studied the American Indian oral tradition (303). The notion of the oral tradition is fascinating to all the directors, though at the end of their first board meeting Ted breaks the "Indian" mystique by showing off to Fannie his wristwatch, which plays the theme music from the *Lone Ranger* television show.

The scenes in which Harold makes his peripatetic presentation are structured around key images and focus on the subversion of invented cultural imagery. The first of these scenes, the urban naming ceremony, takes place at a fry-bread stand. The fry bread, which, as the warrior Plumero whispers to Kingsley, "is white on the inside, you know" (316), represents a mock feast. But the foundation directors are unable to eat what they are offered and the screenplay directs that they "are polite and carry their fry bread to the next scene" (315). The use of Monopoly cards to determine the new names is clearly an ironic comment on the rapacious capitalism that has deprived native communities of their traditional lands (and here Harold's "removal" of the directors from their plush meeting room to a supermarket car park is significant) but it is the receptacle containing the cards that represents the invention of Indian stereotypes. Harold draws each card from what he calls "the cigar store Indian box" (316).

Viewers have been prepared for this icon of the "Indian" by the conversation between Son Bear and Andrew that takes place on the bus ride to the naming ceremony. Andrew asks, hesitantly, how many Indians there were there in the New World at the time of Columbus's discovery. Son Bear replies, "None" and explains in response to Andrew's confusion, "None, not one. Columbus never discovered anything, and when he never did he invented us as Indians because we never heard the word before he dropped by by accident" (314). Realizing his mistaken assumption that native people would answer to the name "Indian," Andrew rephrases his question: "How many tribal people were there here then, ahh, before Columbus invented Indians?" (314). The smug satisfaction is wiped from his face when Son Bear replies, "Forty-nine million, seven hundred twenty-three thousand, one hundred and ninety-six on this continent, including what is now Mexico" (314–15). The camera is directed away from the person of Son Bear to the scene of tribal people at which Andrew is looking through the bus window. The irony of seeing the very kind of tribal people that Son Bear's voice tells us were destroyed is emphasized by Andrew's lame response: "Really, that many then?" (315). This culminates in Ted's question in the final board room scene; he wants to ask about Indian alcoholism but is embarrassed by the insensitivity of his enquiry. He is greatly relieved when the warriors guess what is troubling him and Harold assures him: "Pinch beans are the perfect booze blocker, the beans block the temptation to take alcohol from evil white men" (331). Vizenor's anger at the legacy of genocide and the contemporary devastation of tribal communities surfaces in scenes such as this, but his rage informs even the comic scenes of the drama.

Earlier on the bus ride Andrew asks New Crows for his opinion of the Bering Strait migration theory. New Crows asks in response, "Which way, east or west?" Andrew is perplexed by the possibility of questioning in which direction across the Bering Strait the speculative migration could have occurred. Finally the exchange ends with New Crows informing Andrew, "Jesus Christ was an American Indian" (312), a theme Vizenor explores in detail in his novel *The Heirs of Columbus* (1991). In exchanges like this, the abrupt shift of meaning out of familiar ways of thinking liberate consciousness into new possibilities of perception and understanding. Similarly, when Marion responds to Harold's presentation with incredulity, "Miniature oranges, and now pinch beans, what ever will be next?" (311), Harold is quick to take her rhetorical question seriously: "Truffles and cashews . . . Red Lake truffles . . . Grand Portage cashews. . . . Not to mention White Earth caviar" (311). Harold mixes luxury goods with reservation names to create new possibilities for meaning and new associations with the idea of the "Indian."

The scene set in the Anthropology Department begins with Harold standing on an artifact case while Plumero projects on to his body images of the Ghost Dance. These images change to those of the death scene at Wounded Knee and, finally, to images of a Wild West show. Artificial images of "Indians" are literally projected on to Harold, much to the concern of the foundation directors and the anthropologists who fear the "militants" will seize the tribal artifacts. A news reporter asks whether Harold is staging a protest against the Anthropology Department, but as Harold remarks, "The cultures that anthropologists invent never complain about anything" (323) because they have never existed in reality, only in anthropological discourse. The softball game, which completes the presentation, brings to a culmination this satire of stereotypes. Harold dresses each team, the warriors in shirts that read "Anglos" and the directors in shirts that read "Indians." He instructs each team in tactics, telling the "Anglos" (that is, the warriors), "We're here to win and win big. . . . Play by the rules if you must, but rape and plunder to win the game. . . . When the 'Indians' talk about the earth and their sacred ceremonies, steal a base, win the game like we stole their land, with a smile" (325). He tells the "Indians" (that is, the foundation directors), "The elders said we should never enter the game to win but to dream. . . . We are made in dreams and the white man is the one who must win" (326). Harold swaps between the two shirts, exchanging one identity for another, tricking the "Indians" into positions of victimry while the "Anglos" steal the game.

Throughout the drama we are actively involved in Vizenor's ironic humor as we witness the function of teasing as social control. Through his use of humor, Harold makes the foundation directors do as he wants. Flavia Carreiro identifies three kinds of humor in the screenplay: Indians making fun of themselves, of historical situations, and of Anglos.[19] What is important is that the agents of the dramatic humor are the tribal characters. According to Kimberly Blaeser, the screenplay "reinforces one of the notions most vital in Vizenor's view of Native American culture: survival through wit and humor. It identifies humor as a tool of mediation and a means to achieve balance. It also reinforces the Vizenor truism: 'Humor has political significance' (*Heirs of Columbus*, 166)."[20]

Ishi and the Wood Ducks: Postindian Trickster Comedies (1995)

One of the subtexts to the anthropologists' fear that the Warriors of Orange will attempt to take back the tribal artifacts held in the glass cases of the Department of Anthropology is the anxiety surrounding the issue of repatriation, particularly the return and appropriate interment of native human remains. Vizenor has written passionately on this subject on numerous occasions, often with reference to the figure of Ishi, the Yahi man who lived and, in 1916, died in the Museum of Anthropology at the University of California at Berkeley. The novels *Chancers* and *The Heirs of Columbus* explicitly address the return of native bones; *Crossbloods: Bone Courts, Bingo, and Other Reports* (1990) includes the essays "Bone Courts: The Natural Rights of Tribal

Bones," originally published in *American Indian Quarterly* (1986), and "Socioacupuncture: Mythic Reversals and the Striptease in Four Scenes," which in different form appears as "Graduation with Ishi" in *The Trickster of Liberty*. In the context of her discussion of Vizenor's calls for a "Bone Court," to determine the human rights vested in tribal remains, Juana María Rodríguez describes these tribal remains as "silent witnesses": "metaphors for the lost, stolen, appropriated, displaced and disemboweled narratives of indigenous peoples."[21] In the play "Ishi and the Wood Ducks," however, Ishi is not a silent witness. Vizenor is concerned to give Ishi voice and a vital presence while dramatizing the genocidal trauma and cultural appropriation experienced by Ishi.

In the essay "Ishi Obscura," published in *Manifest Manners*, Vizenor explains: "He is not the obscure other, the mortal silence of savagism and the vanishing race. The other pronoun is not the last crude measure of uncivilization; the silence of that tribal man is not the dead voice of racial photographs and the vanishing pose."[22] With these words, Vizenor challenges the division of "us" versus "him" ("the other pronoun") and the savagery versus civilization assumption separating white from Indian cultures that underlies the use of the pronoun. In Ishi's silence—he spoke his tribal language and learned limited English during his period in the museum—Vizenor wants us to hear presence rather than absence, the presence of the living man rather than the absence of the invented Indian role that Ishi could not play. The reference to racial photographs refers in general to the memorializing efforts of white scholars and journalists but more particularly to the book in which Ishi's photograph appeared, *The Vanishing Race*, compiled by Joseph Kossuth Dixon from the photographs taken by the "Rodman Wanamaker Expedition of

Citizenship to the North American Indian" in 1913. These images sought to record the extinguishing lives of "Vanishing Americans."[23] Although Ishi's image appears in this book, and despite the label attached to him as "the last of his tribe," Vizenor explains that Ishi was not silent and that he told stories as his own form of memorialization. The "Wood Ducks" of the play's title refers to the lengthy and complex stories Ishi loved to tell. But Ishi was powerless to stop the colonialist efforts that recreated him as a doomed victim of history. In Vizenor's reinterpretations of Ishi's history, we find the man of flesh restored in place of the "last primitive," the "last of the stone":

> Ishi told stories to be heard, not recorded and written, he told stories to be heard as the sounds of remembrance, and with a sense of time that would never be released in the mannered silence of a museum. Overnight he became the last of the stone, the everlasting unknown, the man who would never vanish in the cruel ironies of civilization.[24]

Vizenor may be punning here on the tribal significance of stone (the twin brother of Naanabozho, the Anishinaabe tribal trickster, is a stone); as "the last of the stone," Ishi would be the last trickster of his tribe. Ishi was not his name; he never disclosed his real or tribal name. In his tribal language "Ishi" means "one of the people."[25] As Louis Owens has pointed out, the openness of this name offers endless opportunities for self-reinvention: "Vizenor makes it clear that Ishi exists forever in the moment of his stories reinventing himself within the oral tradition with each utterance."[26] In the play Ishi becomes the focus of a complex play of presence and absence. Vizenor explains in an interview: "Ishi is a visionary presence, and at the same time, he is an ethnographic absence. . . . He is a voice of memories, and he is wise, witty, and tricky. Ironically, the other characters are the real absence, as they forever hold to their ethnographic discoveries and documents."[27]

The performance history of the play is quite limited. It was produced as a staged reading directed by Randy Reinholtz by the Red Path Theater Company of Chicago in March 1996, and a production of the play was performed by the Lakeside Theatre at the University of Essex in June 1999. The historical background to the play is recounted by Louis Owens in his essay "The Last Man of the Stone Age: Gerald Vizenor's *Ishi and the Wood Ducks*" (2000). Owens tells how in 1985, while he was a visiting professor of Native American studies at the University of California Berkeley, Vizenor formally proposed that the wing of Dwinelle Hall housing the Native American Studies Department be renamed Ishi Hall. Despite strong student support for the proposal, administrators rejected the idea with a compromise suggestion, that a proposed extension to Kroeber Hall be named in honor of Ishi. This suggestion was rejected by Vizenor as the expression of "a new intellectual colonialism."[28] To recognize Ishi's service to the University of California only through his association with Alfred Kroeber, effectively to memorialize Ishi as an extension of Kroeber, would be a further assertion of Anglo-American dominance through language and the power of discursive relationships. Vizenor could not accept this flawed compromise. In 1992, when Vizenor returned to Berkeley as a tenured full professor, his proposal was resubmitted to coincide with the quincentenary celebrations of Columbus's "discovery" of the New World. In a June 1992 letter to Chancellor Chang-Lin Tien, Vizenor declared that "the very institutions and the foundational wealth of this state are based on stolen land and the murder of tribal people."[29] After much administrative delay another compromise proposal was made, this one to name the central courtyard of Dwinelle Hall "Ishi Court." The dedication ceremony took place on May 7, 1993. Vizenor's address on that occasion included this angry observation: "There is a wretched silence in the histories of this state and nation: the silence of tribal names. The landscapes are burdened with untrue discoveries. There are no honorable shadows in the names of dominance. The shadows of tribal names and stories persist, and the shadows are our natural survivance."[30] The "shadows" to which he refers are the historical figures signified by the names, the "robber barons" whose generous endowments to public institutions obscure not only the sources of their wealth but also the tribal people who were destroyed and yet whose names and stories persist despite efforts to eradicate them.

Vizenor's play addresses the persistence of Ishi's story despite the fact that his tribal name is lost. The drama enacts the Anglo-American metanarrative of race, the ideology of "savagism and civilization," the dynamics of white discursive dominance and of "Indian" victimry. In his extensive "Historical Production" notes, which introduce the text of the play, Vizenor describes the circumstances of Ishi's "discovery" in Oroville, California, on August 29, 1911. He tells the few known details of Ishi's life before he entered white society and briefly explains how Ishi died. It is clear from this brief account that "Ishi" is treated, though not unkindly, as an artifact or object possessed by state agencies. When first discovered he was placed in jail because the sheriff did know what else to do with him. Ishi cannot communicate in English, no one understands his Yahi dialect, and yet he must be placed somewhere. A few days later the anthropologist Alfred Kroeber contacted the police and Ishi was released into Kroeber's custody to live in the Museum of Anthropology, effectively as a living exhibit. Ishi is defined by absence or what is not there: the rest of his tribe (all dead) or the "Indian" characteristics that would be recognizable to his captors. Vizenor quotes at length from the contemporary newspaper report of Ishi's death:

> Ishi, the man primeval is dead. He could not stand the rigors of civilization, and tuberculosis, that arch-enemy of those who live in the simplicity of nature and then abandon that life, claimed him. . . . He furnished amusement and study to the savants of the University of California for a number of years, and doubtless much of ancient lore was learned from him, but we do not believe he was the marvel that the professors would have the public believe. He was just a starved-out Indian from the wilds of Deer Creek who, by hiding in its fastness, was able to long escape the white man's pursuit. And the white man with his food and clothing and shelter finally killed the Indian just as effectually as he would have killed him with a rifle.[31]

In this report Ishi is the "Vanishing American." In Vizenor's quotation of the report, however, Ishi becomes a simulation of the "Indian" created by white America. Ishi is then an example of the lost "Indian" original that in fact never existed. In *Manifest Manners* Vizenor reminds us, "The Indian was an occidental invention that became a bankable simulation; the word has no referent in tribal languages or cultures."[32]

Ishi would not have understood himself as an "Indian," thus the conditions necessary to apply this category label to him is one of Vizenor's concerns in the play. The action begins with a prologue, which is followed by four acts. In the prologue much of the dialogue addresses the importance of names and the process of naming. Ishi and an old woman, Boots, sit on a bench outside a federal courthouse. Their verbal exchange links names with stories: "Indian" is a name within an Anglo-American story of conquest, but it bears no relation to tribal stories; Boots tells how her husband lied about their married name and explains that because her birth records were lost in the war she has no "real" name except her nickname. "Real" names, nicknames, secret sacred names, married names, "museum names"—with this cluster of kinds of naming Vizenor suggests how complicated naming can be. And yet a name is indispensable. Boots explains that she needs a legal name or she faces deportation. Without a name she has no story, no country, and no place. The name given to Ishi by the anthropologists gives him a role in the story of American expansionism, a tribe that has been wiped out, and a place in the museum. In conversation with Vizenor and in the context of the play, Jack Foley comments that "a name is fossilized history."[33] With the name bestowed on Ishi comes a history that is no more of his choosing than the name. Yet this name and this history provide him with visibility, what the character Judge Kroeber in act 4 calls criminal "colonial inventions" (335). Vizenor raises the issue of who has the power to name? Ishi is named by Kroeber with what Ishi refers to as his "museum name"; this question of the legitimacy of bestowing names with the history and authority that accompany them extends to the process of the federal recognition of tribes and of individual membership within the tribe. Vizenor does not underestimate the importance of names but he emphasizes the problematic nature of naming within a colonialist situation.

Ishi is rendered invisible throughout much of the play, except when he is simulating; with the exception of Boots, he can only be seen by the other characters when he is performing the role of an invented "Indian." The dramatic relationship between the characters of Ishi and Boots is very important. The verbal play between them is highly comic, but it also introduces and emphasizes the major themes of the play. These characters function together as a chorus, commenting on the action they witness (along with the audience) and providing alternative contexts for interpreting the dramatic action. They are introduced together as rather ridiculous figures. Ishi is wearing an oversized suit, and as the audience watches, he removes his shoes and socks and inserts leather thongs into his ears. Before the eyes of the audience, he adopts the stereotypical accessories of the "Indian." Elvira Pulitano explains the significance of the characters' appearances: "Ishi is playing the role of the 'funny' man or 'funny' Indian, the leather thongs being signifiers of his Indianness. In the author's humoristic intent, Ishi perfectly embodies the stereotype of the 'Dumb Indian,' an artifact of the Euramerican anthropologists. His matched partner, Boots, who wears 'a floral print dress with white boots and bold accessories,' is brought on stage to complete his personality. She also functions as an accomplice in the act of ridiculing the people associated with the museum."[34]

The Museum of Anthropology provides the setting for act 1, in which the focus now falls upon stories rather than names, or the stories that lend significance to names. Ishi sits at the entrance to his tribal house, the wickiup, and Boots (now the janitor) dusts the floor while she observes and (as prescribed in the stage directions) silently reacts with gestures to the main action. The medical doctor, Saxton Pope, enters and, reminding Ishi of his previous home in the mountains, provokes a disturbing reaction. "The savages, the savages," Ishi whispers. These are not "Indian" savages but the miners who, Ishi tells, "have no stories. . . . [They] are dead voices, no songs, no stories" (307). Here the white "conquerors" are described in terms of absence, as having no stories and no culture. In contrast is Pope's account of Ishi's stories, which are healing the women in the hospital. Ishi resists the visit of the reporter, Ashe Miller, and photographer, Prince Chambers, which Kroeber sees as important to the museum's control of Ishi's public image. The verbal exchange between Ishi and Miller takes place at cross-purposes—she wants confirmation of her stereotypical assumptions about "Indians" and Ishi simply wants her to leave—which reduces the museum staff (Kroeber, Pope, and Waterman the linguist) to laughter, but Boots is disturbed by what she witnesses. Miller and Waterman engage in a further exchange of misunderstanding when she asks the meaning of the word "ulisi." Waterman replies, "I don't understand" and the conversation continues:

> MILLER: How could you not understand ulisi?
> ISHI: Don't understand.
> WATERMAN: "Ulisi" means not to understand.
> MILLER: I understand. (314)

The opacity of language, made clear in this encounter, prevents the understanding and communication that it should facilitate. The reporter and the photographer are determined to understand Ishi as an invented "Indian" despite his resistance. The act concludes with Prince's attempts to photograph Ishi, who refuses to remove his clothes. He whispers to Kroeber, who speaks for him: "Ishi say he not see any other people go without them, without clothes (*Pause*), and he say he never take them off no more" (315). Ishi refuses to participate in what Vizenor has elsewhere termed a "cultural striptease," where he would submit to the pressure of the dominant group to show them what they want to see.[35]

Act 2 is set in the Mount Olivet Cemetery columbarium, seventy years after Ishi's death. Ishi and Boots sit on a bench outside, from where they can comment on the action. In this and the following two acts, Ishi is "a character in the story of his life after his death" (299). As Vizenor specifies in the stage directions, "The actors and names of the characters are the same in the prologue and four acts of the play. The sense of time, manifest manners, and historical contradictions are redoubled and enhanced by the mutations of identities in the same characters" (302). Miller and Prince are present to record the occasion; Angel Day, an expert on tribal histories is there as manager of the cemetery association; and Trope Browne is the cemetery attendant to whom Zero Larkin introduces himself as "native sculptor with a vision" (316). In this act experts and invented "Indians" stage an encounter over the urn containing Ishi's ashes. The "expert" Angel tells stories about Ishi as a shaman and maker of pottery, which are loudly contradicted by Ishi in his verbal exchange with Boots. When Boots comments that Angel has lied, Ishi disagrees because "Angel is an expert on Indians." As he reasons, "Indians are inventions, so what's there to lie about?" (318). Vizenor's most biting satire is reserved, however, for the sculptor Zero Larkin, who claims that "Ishi is a name with sacred power" (319), though Ishi immediately reminds the audience that "Ishi" was never his name. When Ishi calls out, "Zero, do your inspiration thing with my pot" (320), no one hears him (except the audience, who are placed in a position to appreciate the dramatic irony of the situation). When Ishi acts outside the character of an "Indian," he is neither seen nor heard.

The following act takes place in Kroeber Hall, among the members of the Committee on Names and Spaces. Angel is now a professor of anthropology and chair of the committee; Trope Browne, Ashe Miller, Prince Chamber, and Alfred Kroeber are all professors and members of the committee; and Ishi and Boots sit on a bench to the side and are unseen by the committee. The proposal being debated is Kroeber's desire to change the name of Kroeber Hall to either Ishi Hall or Big Chiep Hall, following the nickname Ishi bestowed on him. The terms of the debate put into question relationships of subject and object in the naming process, the distinction between the historical and the ephemeral, and the nature of knowledge and the privileging of Western academic knowledge over tribal epistemologies.

The final act (act 4) is set in a federal courtroom and thus closes the frame opened in the prologue. This setting is one of the structural reversals that Vizenor describes as characteristic of the play. The play opens with Ishi and Boots on a bench outside a federal courtroom and it ends in the "First District Court of Character." Vizenor explains: "Ishi is present and an active character in the prologue, and in the first and last acts. The audience is aware of his ironic presence in the second and third acts, but only his name and ashes in an urn are mentioned by the other characters in the play."[36] In this act Kroeber is the judge who must adjudicate the matter of Ishi's "Indian-ness." Ashe Miller is the prosecutor, Saxton Pope is the defense attorney, Angel Day is the bailiff, Prince Chamber is the court clerk, and the other characters are present as witnesses. The charge is read aloud by the judge: "Mister Ishi has been charged with seven counts of violating provisions of the Indian Arts and Crafts Act of 1990. He sold objects as tribal made, and could not prove that he was in fact a member of a tribe or recognized by a reservation government" (327). As Pulitano observes, "It is not by mere chance that Vizenor sets the main issue of the play in a court. Court cases are cultural definitions, a further attempt by Euramerica to 'establish' and 'define' Indians."[37] The irony is that as the last of his tribe, Ishi has no tribe that could validate his claim to tribal status. Further, the government that demands this kind of proof of him is the government that oversaw the destruction of his community. Ishi's defense is that the Indian-ness he is asked to prove is an identity category invented by Europeans. Ishi fails to conform to the "Indian" identity prescribed by European interpretations of native custom, as when, for example, he makes arrowheads from the glass of broken bottles, a modern survivance practice that contradicts romantic images of Indians derived from a mythic past.

As the play reaches an ending, the audience is placed like a jury in relation to the action. Judge Kroeber makes a direct address, or even appeal, to the audience when he is called upon to formulate a ruling: "What would you do under the circumstances? *Gestures to the audience*" (335). He reduces the issue to a few binaries: "cultural romance" or "consumer fraud"? "legislative protectionism" or "cultural romance"? (335). Finally the judge decides that he cannot make a ruling and instead looks directly at the audience as he says, "Ishi is real and the law is not." He continues, "Therefore, my decision is to declare that the accused is his own tribe. Ishi is his sovereign tribal nation, and this is clear and presents evidence of his character. . . . Ishi, the man so named, has established a tribal character in a museum and in his endless wood duck stories" (336). The judge, and the play, decides in favor of the importance of stories, of oral narratives, and of the storier as a "living character." As Louis Owens remarks, "In *Ishi and the Wood Ducks*, the written advances to the oral, and the co-constructive audience—brought onto the stage by both Ishi and Judge Kroeber—becomes the active jury and is challenged to deconstruct the Indian, to find the lonesome survivor who, in good humor, honored his sacred name and simply called himself 'one of the people.'"[38]

CHAPTER 5

Gerald Vizenor as Novelist and Storier

In the same way that it is problematic to distinguish the fictional from the documentary in Vizenor's work, so it is difficult to separate the novels from the stories. For example, the book *Hotline Healers: An Almost Browne Novel* (1997) is referred to as "stories" in a further subtitle. Diane Glancy, in her review of the book, calls it a "virtual literature of the imaginative. A new genre of amplifiction."[1] Vizenor does follow Anishinaabe tradition by writing about people rather than facts, and a consequence of this is that his episodic novels, like his stories, present character-focused vignettes in a structure that defies orthodox literary categories. *Landfill Meditation: Crossblood Stories* (1991), for instance, focuses on the characters Almost Browne, Bunnie La Pointe, Father Father Mother [*sic*] and the Flat Earth Society, Mildred Fairchild the reservation teacher, Monsignor Lusitania Missalwait, who owns a stretch of interstate toll road and charges white people a dollar to drive on it, and Clement Beaulieu, who narrates several stories, including the title story. In the essay "Native Chance: Clement Vizenor and the Great Depression," included in the collection *Literary Chance* (2007), Vizenor ascribes two primary functions to the characters in his novels: to challenge and subvert the colonialist structures of thought and language that keep native people in a condition of disempowerment and to contradict the stereotypes of native people that also are disempowering and place native people in the oppressed position of "victims." Consequently, as he writes, "survivance, the union of active survival and resistance to cultural dominance, is an obvious spirit of native sovereignty in my novels."[2] We can see this survivance at work in Vizenor's stories as well as his novels. In the eponymous story "Landfill Meditation," for example, Clement Beaulieu tells the story of Martin Bear Charme, a tribal trickster who has obtained a federal loan to buy an area of mud flats, which he fills with waste he hauls from San Francisco. Like a contemporary earthdiver he creates a "landfill reservation" for which he petitions federal recognition as a sovereign nation and against which he contrasts the "old" reservations, where "the tribes were the refuse."[3]

John Purdy proposes that if the epic poem *Bear Island* can be described as a "fifty-page haiku imagistic poem," then Vizenor's novels can be seen as "150-page haiku prose."[4] In response Vizenor remarks on Kimberly Blaeser's scholarly work, which highlights precisely this aspect of Vizenor's novels: where haiku profoundly influences the imagistic texture of his prose. The story "Luminous Thighs," in *Landfill Meditation,* invokes one of Vizenor's best-known haiku poems in the following exchange between Griever de Hocus, the trickster hero of Vizenor's second novel, and a fellow train traveler:

"Haiku," she said and presented her book.
"Fat green flies," Griever responded.
"Square Dance."
"Histories across the grapefruit," he continued.
"Honor your partner," she concluded and clapped her
        hands to celebrate a haiku.[5]

Vizenor comments that the writing of haiku early in his literary career aided his development as a writer because it "taught me

how to hold an imagistic gaze, and that gaze is my survivance.
. . . Many chapters in my novels begin with a natural metaphor
and create a sense of the season, the tease of a haiku scene. I
learned how to create tension in concise images, by the mere
presence of nature."[6] The opening line of Vizenor's first novel,
Bearheart, begins in exactly this imagistic way: "The last full
moon of summer slumps alone through the palmate shadows of
the cedar night and then stretches out over the dark river water
into morning."[7] If we structure the first part of the sentence into
three lines, thus

> The last full moon of summer
> slumps alone through the palmate
> shadows of the cedar night

we have a haiku in the style characteristic of Vizenor's haiku
poems: an opening line that specifies the season, a second line
beginning with a verb, and a third line that introduces a sense of
natural presence as the object of the sentence.

This novel was first published in 1978 as *Darkness in Saint
Louis Bearheart* and was republished in 1990 under the new title
Bearheart: The Heirship Chronicles. In the introduction to *Fugitive Poses*, Vizenor tells of the difficulties he encountered as he
sought to publish the book. First, his New York literary agent
informed him that two publishers had lost his manuscript, and
then, when Vizenor's editor at the *Minneapolis Tribune* sent the
novel to a publisher of his acquaintance, a third copy went missing. Two years later Truck Press agreed to publish the book, but
after typesetting the first few chapters the printers refused to continue on the grounds that the novel was "too obscene and violent." The printer of the second edition in 1990 made the same
objection.[8] In conversation with Louis Owens, Vizenor comments, "I think the people probably threw it away. . . . They

probably read it and thought 'Holy shit,' because it's not any-thing they would expect on an Indian theme."[9] *Bearheart* (as I will refer to the 1990 text) is a disturbing book because it is a radical book. In this novel Vizenor subverts all simulations. He tells how a friend, who had assigned the novel as part of a com-munity college literature course, asked him to visit the class to respond to the students' anger. He points out that the students read his narrative as a representation of the real, as a work of mimesis, while what he is representing in this novel is "an *indian* simulation, a fugitive pose that my novel evaded and decon-structed." He continues: "My first response to the students that morning was a rhetorical question: show me the real violence in trickster stories, and is there anything in *Bearheart* that is not true, that you have not already paid good money to see as enter-tainment in movie theaters, that you have not already seen on television or read in newspapers?"[10] Vizenor's work shocks us out of our complacent acceptance of a certain degree of violence as normative in our society and a learned recognition that vio-lence is acceptable when it is practiced by particular agents. As a result the image of a violent bear is shocking to a socialized human reader but, as Vizenor remarks, the "bears are hunted to extinction, and that is the real act of violence."[11]

The full extent of Vizenor's achievement in *Bearheart* is in-dicated by the comparisons made by critic Bernadette Rigal-Cellard, who sees the novel as essentially a pilgrimage narrative that belongs together with Dante's *Divine Comedy*, Chaucer's *Canterbury Tales*, Boccaccio's *Decameron*, Cervantes' picaresque *Don Quixote*, and, even more, Bunyan's *Pilgrim's Progress*.[12] A. LaVonne Brown Ruoff describes the novel as "a satirical and allegorical epic cycle that combines elements of classical and Western European epics and American Indian oral narratives."[13]

She explains: "Vizenor's descriptions of the four worlds of Indian people combine the emergence and migration myths of Southwestern tribes with the flood myths of Algonkin-speaking tribes. Cedarfair begins his journey in the third world, which evil spirits have filled with contempt for the living and fear of death. He must reach the fourth world, in which these spirits will be outwitted through using the secret languages of animals and birds. Accompanying Cedarfair on his journey is a bizarre collection of followers that represent various figures from Indian mythology as well as human vices and virtues. Episodes in the novel denote stages of the ritual quest and incidents occur without explanation, as they do in American Indian hero cycles."[14] Alan Velie has interpreted the novel as an inversion of the Anglo-American genre of "frontier gothic" fiction. "If the frontier gothic is a romantic novel of terror set in the western wilderness with Indians playing the role of satanic villains," he writes, "*Darkness in Saint Louis Bearheart* is the obverse: it is a novel of horror written from an Indian point of view about a group of Indians forced from the security of their woodland reservation and driven into the civilized west where cowboys, fascists, and other enemies attempt to exterminate them."[15] The horror here, although fictionalized, is not invented. As Jon Hauss comments, "This is a violence we know is in the real history of North America and its indigenous peoples, a federally-sponsored violence which Vizenor presents as having long produced, indeed as continuing to produce, a particularly excessive history of human and natural loss."[16]

The novel presents the reader with an embedded narrative or a story within a story; the narrative of Proude Cedarfair's epic journey is set out in the manuscript "The Heirship Chronicles: Proude Cedarfair and the Cultural Word War," which constitutes the main part of the text. This is preceded by a "Letter to the Reader," which is printed in italic font to set it off typographically from the main text. The "Letter" is written in the first-person mode, beginning "*The bear is in me now.*"[17] Though the identity of the speaker is unknown, we are told two important things in the opening lines. First, "this book" is "*the heirship chronicles on the wicked road to the fourth world,*" which reveals the primary outline of the plot, and second, something terrible, as bad as "*the darkness at the federal boarding school,*" has happened to awaken the "*blood and deep voice of the bear within me*" (vii). As the "Letter" continues, it becomes apparent that the writer is a clerk working for the federal Bureau of Indian Affairs (BIA) and that he is approaching retirement age. During his time working for the BIA, Saint Louis Bearheart (our first-person narrator) has been documenting the sufferings of tribal people at the hands of the federal authorities in what he calls the "heirship stories" or "heirship documents," which he keeps hidden in a filing cabinet in his office. Two motifs are interwoven in the "Letter": Bearheart's recollections of earlier moments when he has experienced transformation into a crow or a bear and his encounter with the young militant woman Songidee during the occupation of the federal building by members of the American Indian Movement.

Songidee enters Bearheart's office, where he is trying to protect the heirship documents. Bearheart is possessed by the voice of the bear, but Songidee "*has little white chickens in her heart*" (ix). She is searching for "*the hairships*" and "*the hairship man*" (x), not knowing what in fact it is that she seeks. She is motivated by a commitment to "Indians" and other "terminal creeds," telling Bearheart, "We have occupied this building in the name of the tribes and the trail of broken treaties . . . and the government will answer all of our demands or else we have come

here to die together for our freedom" (xi), her readiness to embrace suicide is reminiscent of Vizenor's description of AIM militants who also were ready to die for tribal people and their treaty
rights at Cass Lake. Songidee brings into his office the "*new
tribal evils*" that Bearheart has told the reader he fears: plastic
bear claws, colored chicken feathers, and the dead words that
suggest "*tribal imagination and our trickeries to heal are in
ruin*" (ix). When challenged by Bearheart, "*she smiles, proud to
hold freedom in terminal creeds*" (xi). The verbal exchange
between Songidee and Bearheart sets the stage for Vizenor's
deconstruction of "Indian" stereotypes that are embraced by
contemporary native people. Bearheart reports her militant
speech: "*We took this building for tribal people, for our past and
present on the reservations, says the bare chicken. We are the
new warriors out for tribal freedom, but you old fuckers sold out
to the white man too long ago to understand the real movement*" (xiii).

The phrase "bare chicken" is revealing in its context: Bearheart's "Letter to the Reader" contains very little description and
comprises a great deal of direct reported speech, which is set
down typographically with no quotation marks and no attribu-
tive tags. The result is that the reader can identify the speaker of
each utterance only by context and by alternation—since two
characters are speaking, generally they take turns to speak. But
we are given very few clues about the action that accompanies
this verbal exchange. At some point Bearheart seduces Songidee,
and by the end of the "Letter" they are engaged in sexual inter-
course. But where did the seduction begin? Shortly before
Songidee's militant speech we read:

> *Songidee she is passive.*
> *Tender breasts in the darkness.*

> *Listen, ha ha ha haaaa.*
> *White Indian she shouts and unbuttons*
> *her leather blouse.* (xii)

Which of these words are directed at the reader, which are reported as spoken dialogue, and which are interior monologue remains ambiguous. Does Bearheart only think to himself "*Tender breasts in the darkness*"? Or does Songidee begin to remove her clothes in response to him speaking this line? And when Bearheart describes her as a "bare chicken" does this mean that she has now removed all her clothes? Or is Vizenor, through Bearheart, punning on the homonym bare/bear to suggest the sexual union that is implicit but will soon become explicit in the text? By using indirection in this way, Vizenor draws attention to the various forms in which communication can take place as a prelude to Songidee's reading of Bearheart's "heirship documents," which brings us to the main narrative. Certainly her attitude begins to change after this verbal exchange with Bearheart, when she stops dismissing him as "*White Indian*"; instead, suspecting that he is not what she had assumed, she asks him, "*Where did you come from old man?*" (xiii), and finally, while they are having sex, she addresses him as "*old bear*" (xiv).

Bearheart describes the heirship chronicles to Songidee as a book about "sex and violence" (xiii). However, the main narrative begins, in haiku fashion, with a powerful image of "the last full moon of summer" (5) setting over a river as the sun rises. This is important because the novel will end with a similar image of the solstice sunrise, the moment at which Proude Cedarfair transforms into a bear and "soars through stone windows" (5). It is precisely a stone window on a winter solstice morning that will offer him access to the fourth world, where, leaving behind the third world that we now inhabit, "evil spirits are outwitted in the secret languages of animals and birds" (5). This first chapter, "Morning Prelude," introduces the crucial mystical dimension of the quest related in the main narrative. It is in the second chapter, "Cedar Celebrants," that the sex and violence begins. Here the narrator relates the stories of the ancestors whose legacy of resistance Proude Cedarfair continues. These three ancestors "defended their sovereign circle from national and tribal governments, from missionaries, treekillers, and evil tribal leaders. Seven sons have died defending the sacred nation. One son in every generation has survived to protect the dominion of natural cedar" (7). The stories of their struggles are violent; the death of First Proude Cedarfair's mixed-blood wife combines the sex and violence to which Bearheart refers.

Fourth Proude Cedarfair is the protagonist of the novel. A trickster figure, he survives by his wits rather than by physical violence through the latest challenge to his cedar nation. In the fictional world of *Bearheart*, gasoline and fuel oil reserves have been exhausted through political mismanagement and the federal government is now looking to tribal timber as an energy source. As a result the federal agents Proude first encounters travel by bicycle. They are frightened away by Proude's threatening bear voices but they run to Jordan Coward, the corrupt drunken reservation president, whose enmity toward the Cedarfairs brings him into agreement with the interests of the federal government. Knowing Coward's desire for revenge, which he could achieve by assigning the cedar nation to the federal demand for trees, Proude realizes that the only way to defend the ancient cedar trees is by leaving them and the nation. Without the Cedarfairs he hates so passionately, Proude reasons, Coward will have no motive to destroy the trees. Thus Proude and his wife Rosina, along with the seven crows who accompany him, are driven from their woodland reservation.

The theme of transformation is prominent in the narrative from the start and, as the story develops, Vizenor explores gender, sexual, and animal/human forms of transformation. The narrative begins with transformation: Proude changes into a bear to scare away the federal agents. As Bernadette Rigal-Cellard explains, "Proude Cedarfair exemplifies this process best. . . . He can turn into a bear on a whim and must be understood as an avatar of the trickster Naanabozho, and also of *gichimakwa* . . . , the great bear of the myth who is but the medicine boy who can resurrect the sick and teaches the secrets of the *midewiwin,* the secret society of the Chippewa. He was begotten by an Anishinaabe woman impregnated by the sun on the asking of the *manidoog* (the spirits) to save mankind from diseases and death: 'I am a *manidoo* and can take any form I wish, I came on earth to teach you what I was sent among you for' (*Summer in the Spring* 89–92)."[18] In her 2002 essay "Postmodern Bears in the Texts of Gerald Vizenor," Nora Baker Barry has provided a comprehensive account of the importance of bear characters in Vizenor's fiction up to *Dead Voices* (1992). She treats Vizenor's use of the bear motif under the various headings of spiritual, erotic, and literary bears. Linking each aspect of the bear figure is the role played by this important spiritual guide in the Anishinaabe *midewiwin* or Grand Medicine Society, also referenced by Rigal-Cellard: "In the rituals of the Grand Medicine Society, bears serve as guides, barriers, the breaker of barriers, and guardians of portals to spiritual power."[19] This helps to account for the importance of windows in *Bearheart*: Proude and Rosina escape Coward's murderous rage by secretly leaving their cabin through the window, and Proude enters the fourth world through a stone window at the end of the novel.

Not all bears are the transcendent mystical figures Proude represents. The character of Zebulon Matchi Makwa (Wicked Bear) in *Bearheart*, and in the story "Mother Earth Man and Paradise Flies" in *Wordarrows*, represents what Nora Baker Barry describes as all that middle-class society fears of the animal, not so much the potential for violence as the overpowering odors and inescapable corporeality of the animal's physical reality.[20] This figure compels people to become what they fear and so to overcome their fears, and in this way he fulfils the bear's potential to break down social barriers, which in Matchi Makwa's case "often are associated more with class than with race or gender."[21] In *Bearheart* Matchi Makwa dies as a result of his surrender to his lustful obsession with the witch he should be rescuing from the Fast Food Fascists.

Zebulon Matchi Makwa is one of the twelve pilgrims or "apostles" who join the group, under the leadership of Proude, accompanied by animals and birds such as the seven crows. Alan Velie offers a succinct description of the pilgrims as including "Sun Bear Sun, a 300 pounder who carries a small white woman, Little Big Mouse, in a holster at his belt; Benito Saint Plumero, an Anishinaabe clown who has done time in jail for murdering his rival for the favors of a bronze statue; Belladonna Darwin Winter Catcher, the daughter of a white reporter and Lakota holy man who met at the occupation of Wounded Knee; and Lilith Mae Farrier, a white woman who worked as a teacher on a reservation until the tribal elders raped her and their wives ran her off in disgust. To console herself she took two boxers— dogs, not athletes—as lovers."[22] As this list suggests, the pilgrims who accompany Proude on his quest are outcasts, survivors, occupants of the "scapehouse for weirds and sensitives" (35) where Proude and Rosina first take refuge after leaving the reservation for the town. Lilith Mae was molested as a child by her stepfather; Sister Willabelle's body is all scars from the plane crash in the jungle and her two-week ordeal to reach a village; and Benito Saint Plumero, whose oversized nose, feet, and penis render him a collage of clowns, was crippled by loneliness until he discovered the women of the scapehouse. Bernadette Rigal-Cellard explains that "the parody contained in his name is double: Big Foot is also the English name of the great Chippewa war chief Ma-mong-e-se-da. Such a noble name now designates a clown, a freak, the mixed-blood heir of a bigfooted political exile and explorer, Giacomo Constantino Beltrami. Bigfoot's gigantic penis, so appreciated by female, transsexual, and homosexual partners, is derisively called President Jackson to mock, of course, the arch villain of nineteenth-century federal Indian policy."[23]

The theme of transformation is continued in the scapehouse, where all the occupants, including animals, birds, and humans, become after their death food for the living: "The women eat what is known, what and who is part of their lives in the scapehouse, the plants and animals, and so their lives are continued in cellular consciousness of the living energies in the scapehouse" (37). So the dead transform the living and find a form of immortality through cannibalism. The idea of transformation is also explored through the characters' use of masks, particularly Bishop Omax Parasimo, whose use of "metamasks" allows him to become variously Sister Eternal Flame, one of the founders of the scapehouse; Scintilla Shruggles, a "new" pioneer woman; and Princess Gallroad, the hitchhiker. The theme of transformation is linked to that of self-invention when Parasimo lends his meta-masks to his companions. This use of masks to complicate the notion of identity is contrasted with the masks worn by the victims of chemically induced cancer, the "no faces":

> Muscles and flesh twitched and quivered behind the plastic facial features. Eyeballs bulged without skin cover. Teeth were exposed like those of hideous skeletons. The plastic faces were formed with short clinical smiles. Some plastic faces had small paper stars attached to the cheeks and foreheads. . . . Belladonna looked into the faces of the skin cancer victims and then turned away. She could tell who was smiling and frowning from the combination of muscle movements which were visible beneath the transparent plastic masks. First Doctor Wilde and then Justice Pardone turned from the nine faces and retched. (149)

Although some of the pilgrims are repelled by the "no faces," Little Big Mouse is inspired to tell them "stories about her incomplete lives," whipping the "cripples and cancer people" (150) into an orgy of lust and violence that ends with the rape and dismemberment of Little Big Mouse. She is literally transformed into the state of incompletion that she claims to love in those deformed victims of a dying chemical civilization.

The central transformative encounter in the narrative is Proude's struggle with the evil Gambler, a figure of supernatural evil who, in Anishinaabe mythology, challenges the trickster Naanabozho for the souls of the people. Proude does battle with the Gambler in the form of Sir Cecil Staples, who controls the supply of gasoline in a nation without energy resources. The "large sign of the evil gambler" (102) announces in the manner of a theatrical spectacle:

SIR CECIL STAPLES
The Monarch of Unleaded Gasoline
and
The Mixedblood Horde of Mercenaries
Presenting
LIVING OR DYING FOR GASOLINE
Gamble for Five Gallons
NEW TRAPS AND OLD TORTURES
Follow the Rows of Abandoned Cars to the Altar Trailers
OPEN FOR EVIL BUSINESS (103)

Sir Cecil is the antihero; his story of displacement and dispossession provides a parallel with that of Proude. As a child he was abducted by a woman who had been forcibly sterilized by the federal government for having children while on welfare. She takes to driving around the country in her trailer, kidnapping children from shopping malls. As Rigal-Cellard points out, this represents another road narrative within the main road narrative, a criminal parody of Proude's pilgrimage and, like the pilgrims of the Cedarfair caravan, the children learned to love one another: "We learned that biological families are not the center of meaning and identities."[24] But families in Vizenor's writing are complex and ambiguous units of socialization. "Mother," as the Gambler learns to call this woman, encouraged her abducted children to do whatever gave them pleasure: "She said we should feel no guilt, ignore the expectations of others and practice to perfection whatever you choose to do in the world" (126). The Gambler chose killing and death. When Mother found out about his first murder, "she stopped the truck right on the interstate to celebrate the event" (126). Sir Cecil is, on the one hand, a criminal sociopath; on the other hand, to his character is attributed mystical significance as the mythical Gambler. He rationalizes his role as indispensable for the balance of spiritual forces in the world but describes elegiacally the usurpation by government and business the role of evil in bringing death. In this world devastated by economic collapse and government malfeasance, social control has failed and everyone has become a killer. Sir Cecil tells how industrial pollution taught him about slow torture and explains that when the government sanctioned death by industrial poisoning people ceased to care about death: Evil had lost its force. Consequently he confesses, "I am less interested in perfection . . . less interested in death but I still find good times in balancing the world with evil" (126).

Despite these rationalizations the effect of Vizenor's graphic descriptions of the deaths suffered by Sir Cecil's victims emphasizes his evil quality. Sir Cecil challenges his victims to gamble their lives for five gallons of gasoline; when they lose they may choose the manner of their deaths. As Proude enters Sir Cecil's trailer, he sees hanging from the ceiling a pair of skeletons intertwined: a couple who chose strangulation while engaged in the sexual act. Lilith Mae Farrier is challenged too, and although Proude gambles his own life for the return of hers, she sets herself on fire with gasoline. The grisly detail of this scene, such as the narrator's observation that "her thin forearm burned through at the elbow" (135), underlines the horror of her death. Ironically, in the previous chapter, and while Lilith Mae was preparing her self-immolation, Proude challenged the Gambler and, in a repetition of Naanabozho's tricky maneuver, whistled in such a way that Sir Cecil's toss of the dish failed and the figures fell. In the manner of the Anishinaabe story, although the evil Gambler has been defeated, evil has not been destroyed. As they play, Proude and Sir Cecil discuss the nature of good and evil. Sir Cecil claims that the outcome of their wager is irrelevant:

"Evil will still be the winner because nothing changes when good and evil are tied in a strange balance" (131). This is one of the reasons the narrative does not end with the defeat of the evil Gambler. Proude has gambled and won, but he still must find a way to leave behind this devastated third world and discover an access into the fourth.

The conclusion of the novel indeed repeats the key images of the narrative's opening—the stone window, the winter solstice—but now the setting is Pueblo Bonito in the Southwest rather than the woodlands of northern Minnesota. Bradley John Monsma, in his essay "Liminal Landscapes: Motion, Perspective, and Place in Gerald Vizenor's Fiction," notes that the ending of the narrative appropriates a traditional Southwest origin myth: "Expelled from the soon-to-be-logged woodland, Proude Cedarfair and his wife Rosina journey along the empty freeways of an expired world with their mongrels and clown crows. As they travel southwest, they gather the wounded from a spent civilization, finally arriving at the fictional Walatowa Pueblo near a stone arch—the vision window to the next world. N. Scott Momaday's novel *House Made of Dawn* ends in a similar landscape with the mixedblood Abel running in a ceremony that reintegrates him into tribal life and confirms his place in the landscape. Vizenor ends *Bearheart* by appropriating a native Southwest emergence myth. Proude Cedarfair and a trickster companion float through the vision window into the next world."[25]

These intertextual references Vizenor combines with the Anishinaabe earthdiver myth of the novel's opening and various other narrative referents such as European quest narratives. Monsma goes on to highlight the parodic relation between the novel and narratives of American westward expansion: "In the traditional story of the American frontier, seeking elbow room and lighting out for territories free from physical and psychological constraint end in the discovery of new places in a wilderness made visible and substantive only when molded to values of production. Vizenor's parody reorients the frontier and questions the notion of discovery by reintroducing the mythic contexts of people who already live there."[26] The concept of "home" is then placed into question and the constant movement of the characters weakens the connection between place and home. Rosina explains to the Luminous Augur, the character who will pilot them across the Canadian River in western Oklahoma, "We are seeking nothing more than a place to dream again" (210), but Rosina is corrected by the Augur, who tells her that "dreams are not places . . . the places we have known move in dreams" (210). This corrective helps to explain why Rosina is unable to accompany her husband as he transforms his physical shape and departs for the fourth world that exists in his vision but not in any place that can be located here in the dying third world.

Even the deathliness of the present world is placed into question in the narrative. Although the human world is coming to an end, poisoning and devastating much of the natural world as a consequence, still Vizenor is attentive to the resilience of nature, separate from humanity: "Since the end of gasoline, weeds were growing over the asphalt roads. Tough flowers crept over the unused shoulders of the road and sprouted from cracks and potholes. . . . In time trees would take root and turn the cement and asphalt to dust again" (51). What from a human point of view seems to be irreversible destruction is, seen from a different point of view, a process of transformation, of destruction and reconstruction.

Vizenor's novel *Griever: An American Monkey King in China* (1990) is also a trickster narrative, but in this novel Vizenor underlines the similarities between the Anishinaabe trickster and the Chinese Monkey King. As he tells A. Robert Lee, "They were both conceived in stone and create fantastic stories of liberation and survivance. These tricksters ducked the censures of missionaries, anthropologists, and commie revisionists."[27] This connection between Anishinaabe and Chinese cultures is also established in *The Trickster of Liberty: Tribal Heirs to a Wild Baronage* (1988), which celebrates the one hundredth anniversary of the unveiling of the Statue of Liberty in New York yet also anticipates the erection of the Statue of Liberty in Tiananmen Square in Beijing. One of the many narrative threads concerns relations between China and the community of Anishinaabe tricksters, led by Stone Columbus, located at the Barony of Patronia on the White Earth Reservation, where a new tribal nation has been declared. Characters are also shared across these narratives: Griever de Hocus, of course; Sister Eternal Flame; and Mouse Proof Martin, who also appears in *The Trickster of Liberty* and *Earthdivers*. *Bearheart* (1978/1990), *Earthdivers* (1981), and *Griever* (1990) all share characters—who later appear in *The Heirs of Columbus* (1991) and *Hotline Healers* (1997). The effect of the reappearance of the same character in texts that are separated in time is to endow these characters with an ontology that exceeds the reality of any single text. The characters appear to exist outside their textual representations so that each text is an instance of the character rather than the original creation of that character and relations among the recurring characters are complicated and enriched with every iteration.

Vizenor's interest in cultural and historical parallels between Native American, particularly Anishinaabe, cultures and China is explored by Linda Lizut Helstern in two excellent essays: "Blue Smoke and Mirrors: Griever's Buddhist Heart" (1997) and "*Griever: An American Monkey King in China*: A Cross-Cultural Re-membering" (2000). Helstern summarizes: "Vizenor is, of course, a mixedblood member of the Minnesota Chippewa, and his choice of protagonist—a mixedblood trickster-teacher from the White Earth Reservation—underscores the parallels that can be drawn between Native Americans and the Chinese in their historic relationships with the Western imperial powers, including the forced cession of land, the missionaries' role in introducing Western culture, a legacy of racism, and the brutal suppression of a religious and artistic heritage spanning thousands of years."[28] Her remarks here indicate the broad context of common historical experience within which Vizenor identifies points of specific commonality between China and the Anishinaabe, such as the important mythological figure of the trickster and themes like that of transformation leading to enlightenment, which I will discuss below.

In her later essay Helstern addresses the theoretical Asian origin of Native American peoples. She turns to the proposal that if historically Asian migrants crossed the Bering land bridge from Asia to North America, becoming then Native Americans, then Griever's journey to China is in the nature of a homecoming.[29] Vizenor makes a similar suggestion in *Harold of Orange*, for example, when Andrew, one of the directors of the Bily Foundation, asks New Crows about the Bering Straits migration theory and is asked in response whether he means that this theoretical migration took place from Asia to America or vice versa. The novel *The Heirs of Columbus* takes its title from the proposition that Columbus was a descendant of Mayans who migrated to Europe; like his ancestors, the descendants or "heirs" that Columbus left in the Americas are native people. The question of transnational relations between the Americas and Asia, and the Americas and Europe, recurs in Vizenor's work through the trope of homecoming even when, as in *The Heirs of Columbus*, it is the bones and not the person of Pocahontas, repatriated from England, that come home.

Even more than the common experience of European imperialism shared by the Chinese and Native Americans, Vizenor highlights in *Griever* and elsewhere similarities between Buddhist and tribal understandings of the sanctity of life. In *Bearheart* Proude objects to eating kittens because the animals were not honored before they were slaughtered; in *Griever* the trickster hero frees the frogs that are to be dissected in a biology class and later famously frees the chickens that are to be butchered in the marketplace. From these experiences, as Helstern comments, the "White Earth trickster-teacher early understood his bodhisattva role—that not all beings, or even most, are willingly liberated."[30] I will return to the theme of liberation, but here it is interesting to note Vizenor's attitude toward nonhuman nature and animals in particular. The novel *Dead Voices* (1992), for example, comprises a series of stories told by Bagese, a tribal trickster woman who has been transformed into a shamanic bear, and conveyed to us by a first-person narrator. Bagese's stories concern the liberation of animals in an urban environment, and she insists that the narrator tell these stories orally by releasing the voices of animals held within himself. Of course the narrator must betray this promise in order to present us with the written narrative that we are reading. The novel enacts the wanaki game, the game of cards, that Bagese plays each morning: "She turned seven cards in the game, one each for the bear, beaver, squirrel, crow, flea, praying mantis, and the last was the trickster figure, a wild card that transformed the player into an otter, a rabbit, a crane, spider, or even a human."[31] She concentrates on her chosen card and then becomes the stories told through her by the animal depicted. However, the first story that follows the narrator's introduction of Bagese and the wanaki game is titled "Stones" and recounts the origin of Naanabozho and his trickster siblings. It is his brother, Stone, who creates nature and invents the wanaki game to preserve his memory and his presence in the world. Each of the stories that follows enacts the adoption of an animal identity and focalizes the story through that animal consciousness.

His treatment of animals sets Vizenor apart from many contemporary writers, including Native American writers who are often considered in proximity to ideas of nature and animals. In his essay "Authored Animals: Creature Tropes in Native American Fiction," Vizenor writes about the issue of anthropomorphism in the literary representation of animals: "Native American Indians are commonly perceived as being in close association with nature and the natural presence of animals; these associations are sources of native omniscience and consciousness. The literary interpretations of this presence have presumed the doctrines of nativism, animism, naturalism, realism, and other theories."[32] While acknowledging the diverse ways in which animals appear—the "authored animals in literature are wild tropes, fantastic creatures, and others are mundane similes of domestication"—Vizenor remarks on the manner in which stories told about animals tame and restrict them, denying the existence of distinct forms of animal consciousness.[33] It is in this connection that Vizenor develops in this essay a distinction between "generic animals" and "authored animals." In texts where animals are used to generate part of the figurative texture of the work, through phrases such as "he works like a dog" or "she has the sight of an eagle," the animal is reduced to what

Vizenor calls "a generic and literal simile."[34] In contrast he writes, "The authored animals in their novels are both mythic and mundane; the metaphors and similes of animal creations are as diverse as the authors. . . . The authored animals are connected to the environment, not to the similes of human consciousness."[35] An example of Vizenor's "authored animals" is his creation of canine characters, mongrels, such as Pure Gumption the shaman mongrel or Chicken Lips and White Lies in *The Trickster of Liberty*. In *Hotline Healers* White Lies is among the mongrel characters, who also include "Ritzy . . . the first mongrel to drive an automobile. Later he was an instructor at the Animosh Driving School."[36] The point is that Vizenor's dogs do not serve as animated figures of speech that illuminate only aspects of human characters; these dogs are characters in themselves with intrinsic forms of consciousness that render them unique as characters. They are agents, and sometimes leaders, in the narrative action.

Griever de Hocus, though he becomes the trickster Monkey King, remains a human character and must be prepared for his mythical role. In the course of the narrative, Griever meets four trickster-teachers. The first is Wu Chou, the warrior clown who dresses Griever for his Monkey King role; his second teacher is Shitou, the stone shaman who, in Anishinaabe mythology, is the stone brother of Naanabozho; and his third is Hua Lian, who poses like a character from classical Chinese opera. Linda Helstern provides a brief but informative account of the extent to which the secondary characters of the novel conform to the stock characters of the Chinese opera. Egas Zhang, for example, is "a *ching*, the type of the crafty and evil minister"; his unfilial daughter is a *hua dan* or fallen woman; Hua Lian's gold and silver makeup signifies her status as a *ching* or supernatural being;

and Hester's mixed-blood sister, Zhang's obedient daughter Kangmei, is a *ch'ing-i*, but she is also characterized by her name, which means "strong and beautiful."[37] The final trickster-teacher encountered by Griever is Yaba Gezi, the mute pigeon. On Obo Island, Yaba Gezi presents Griever with two mirrors in which he can recall the dream that unifies and motivates the narrative. This dream is first told in a letter written by Griever and addressed to China Browne. In the dream Griever sees bears in the mountains: a fire bear that transforms into a small terracotta humanoid figure and a fire bear wearing a black opal ring set with azure blue stones and a small blue rabbit on a necklace. In his dream he is led past a series of murals at the end of which is a stone man with butterflies on his hands who, with a bear woman, fathered generations of tribal healers across the world. Baskets of bear bones, blue stones, and manuscripts that tell the histories of shaman bear cultures present themselves in Griever's dream. He is required to choose one manuscript and finds that it is marked in the same way as tribal medicine scrolls from the reservation; after reading the stories of the past but before the stories of the future, Griever dreams himself asleep in his dream and, when he awakes, the birchbark manuscript is gone. The search for the birchbark scroll, with its histories of the future, provides much of the impetus for the novelistic plot.

As elsewhere in Vizenor's work, *Griever* is concerned with ontological transformations among animals and humans, dreaming and waking, imagination and reality. The theme of dream and waking realities, and the relations between them, is introduced through the motif of Griever's dream. As the narrative progresses the imagistic elements of the dream manifest themselves in Griever's waking experience: the rabbit pendant, the black opal ring, the luminous blue stones, the old man with butterflies, and the birchbark scroll and its historical contents. This transformation in the ontological realm is represented through transformation on the level of the narrative's own internal ontologies. Stories become real and realities become stories as the narrative progresses. After the death of Hester Hua Dan, Hua Lian tells the story of Rabbit's self-sacrifice to feed the hungry shaman bear; Rabbit is then honored by being transformed into the moon and is from then on known as Jade Rabbit. Hester is found to be wearing the jade rabbit pendant around her neck when she is pulled from the lake. When Griever reaches the body, "he loosened the blue stone rabbit, washed her hair back, raised her face to the moon, touched the scar, and kissed her bloated cheeks."[38] Thus the pendant of Griever's dream becomes an object in the waking world, and the woman wearing the pendant becomes a character of myth, a myth that is told, as Linda Helstern points out, in hybrid form: Vizenor attributes the role of Buddha in the Chinese version of the myth to the shaman bear, thus introducing a key element of Anishinaabe mythology.[39]

The theme of transformation is linked to the novel's other dominant theme: liberation. As Helstern argues, "Liberation becomes both a motive and a motif. The transformation of Griever the trickster-teacher into the American Monkey King turns on the crux of liberation."[40] Liberation is both political, as in the episodes such as Griever's freeing of the prisoners who have been condemned to death or his substitution of the patriotic Chinese anthem "The East Is Red" with the American "Semper Fidelis" and "The Stars and Stripes Forever," and also metaphysical or ontological, a freeing from the literal, physical reality of the everyday into a realm of enlightenment.

In the chapter "Execution Caravan," Griever takes control of the truck transporting eight bound and heavily guarded prisoners to their deaths. He drives to an abandoned warehouse and there unties the prisoners. However, the prisoners react very differently to this sudden freedom: "The three rapists escaped on a small river boat, the heroin dealer brushed his hair and wandered down the bund, the one murderer walked back to the main road, but the prostitute, the robber, and an art historian who exported stolen cultural relics remained on the back of the truck with the mind monkey" (153). These three remaining characters are afraid of their freedom. The prostitute is convinced by her past experiences that freedom is not possible for anyone; the robber is mute and the art historian suggests that his voice has already died. This historian begins to move away from the truck but the spectacle of the rapists being shot by soldiers who fire on their boat is enough to send him rushing back to his seat, where he waits with his hands folded. This gesture of child-like obedience is highly ironic: the historian is obedient to the authority that will kill him, too, and soon enough. Griever demonstrates that freedom is possible in his subversion of governmental authority. However, the fear of liberation afflicts even Griever's Chinese lover, Hester Hua Dan. She confesses to her fear of her father and of public opinion. She is tortured by her father's demand that she abort her child, and she refuses Griever's plans for escape: she says no to the prospect of traveling to Macau and she again says no to the microlight aircraft that can take them away. Ultimately she is also unable to resist Griever's insistence and so tells him that her fear is of flying "but held back the real reason: her fear, resignation to paternal power, and her dedication to the nation" (200). Hester finally loses her life to her fear of freedom; by refusing to meet Griever and spend the night with him, she makes herself available at home to become the victim of her abusive father's murderous rage.

The novel concludes with another letter from Griever to his sister China Browne in which he describes his flight from Tianjin to Macau in the microlight aircraft accompanied by the Sino-American mixed-blood woman Kangmei and the rooster Matteo Ricci, who has accompanied him through many of the narrative episodes. This narrative situation has already been confirmed in the earlier novel, *The Trickster of Liberty* (1988), when the narrator tells us, "China . . . wrote when she was in the People's Republic of China that Griever de Hocus had vanished; he was last seen in the air, over a water park, the police reported, with a rooster and a small blonde."[41] Kangmei's American father has given her one of the sacred bear scrolls, which turns out to contain recipes for dishes such as blue chicken with blueberries and blue mountain corn but not for immortality. Matteo Ricci, as Helstern remarks, is associated with sexuality in both Eastern and Western cultures; the cock links Griever to life, death, time, and history.[42] "Time and space remained . . . something of an illusion to the Chinese until the arrival of the Jesuit missionary Matteo Ricci in 1582," she explains. "Thoroughly versed in Chinese language and civilization, Ricci used Western technical achievements to gain the respect of the Chinese bureaucrats. It was he who brought the first clock, the Western Wheel of Becoming, and the first map of the world to China."[43] But Griever is entirely hostile toward the regulation of life by clocks and other external measures of experience. He recalls telling one of his fellow passengers on the flight to China that "imagination is the real world, all the rest is bad television" (28). In China he finds himself in a culture where experience is regulated differently, apart from the clocks and maps that codify Western lives. In his concluding letter to China Browne he describes an incident that occurs during the microlight flight when they ask for directions: "The real joke is that people never ask directions over here, this is not a map place where people remember an abstract location. We are the map people, not them. We were lost and asked them to make a map in their heads to tell us where they were so we could find out where we were. They know where they are, but we are up in the air" (231). Ironically they need directions to find their way to "freedom in the old colony of Macau" (231), but the journey itself (both the flight and the narrative) has brought Griever to a place where, as he writes China, "I am in my own painting over the mountains" (233). Griever has become an agent in his own birchbark scene, in his own future history. Rather than direct his rage into panic holes dug in the ground and buried there, he has found a way to release his voice and roars his anger into the air.

The seemingly open-ended quality of the conclusion is put into question by Linda Lizut Helstern's attention to the temporal structure of the novel. As she points out, Vizenor's symbolic use of the seasonal cycle suggests completion and closure. The novel's action takes place between the summer solstice and the autumn moon festival, the only Chinese holidays that commemorate historical political protests.[44] The titles Vizenor has given to each of the four sections of the novel are taken from the Chinese lunar calendar: "*Xiazhi:* Summer Solstice," "*Dashu:* Great Heat," "*Bailu:* White Dew," and "*Quifen:* Autumn Equinox." "*Xiazhi:* Summer Solstice," the time of the garlic harvest, is noted with reference to the liberation of garlic (53). "*Dashu:* Great Heat" becomes a time of erotic heat as Griever consummates his relationship with Hester. "*Bailu:* White Dew" is a time of energetic work, which Griever devotes to the effort of freeing the condemned prisoners from the execution caravan. And finally "*Quifen:* Autumn Equinox," a time of celebration, is reversed; as Helstern comments, "Vizenor, characteristically, celebrates it with a trickster reversal, making the celebration a time of deep sorrow."[45] The seemingly indeterminate ending of *Griever* is in fact closed through the gesture to China Browne's letter in *The Trickster of Liberty* and through Vizenor's use of time as a structuring principle of the narrative.

Immediately preceding the final letter, *Griever* concludes with the death of Hester Hua Dan and Hua Lian's recounting of the story of the jade rabbit. Griever rejects the spiritual optimism of the story, shouting, "The revolution ended that jade rabbit monkey shit." He invokes another story, that of the immortal Wu Gang who was instructed that in order to win his freedom he must cut down the cassia tree. But, Griever informs us, "one more wild *but*, . . . the blows were futile, the tree healed faster than he cut" (228). Griever moves away to scream his anger and grief into a hole, a "panic hole," in the earth. He expresses his frustration in the face of a totalized form of socialization that will not allow even the woman who loves him to follow his example of liberation. As quickly as Griever subverts the status quo, the authorities act to annul his subversion. These authorities act most powerfully through the internalized motives and conscience of individuals such as Hester. The ending of the novel is then carefully balanced between the hope of liberation represented by the trickster and the refusal of liberation by those who are too afraid to embrace their own liberty. This balance is however nuanced by the violence of Hester's death and Griever's reaction to this loss.

The representation of violence has been an issue in Vizenor's writing, and for his readers, since the publication of *Bearheart*. In a 1981 interview, and referring primarily to responses to that novel, Vizenor described to Neal Bowers and Charles Silet his discomfort with the denial of violence in contemporary American culture: "Any expressions that are connected to intense human emotions, or rage, which are all a part of living, are denied. I think the way this culture works is dangerous. To deny violence is to create victims, ultimate victims, people who can be controlled merely by the symbolic appearance of violence. Because to deny violence, to control people, all one needs to do is suggest violence."[46] In his 2003 novel *Hiroshima Bugi: Atomu 57*, Vizenor offers some of his most radical thinking on the difficult twinned issues of violence and peace.

Hiroshima Bugi is narrated in thirteen chapters, each divided into two halves that alternate between two narrators, Ronin Ainoko Browne, a *hafu* or mixed-blood Japanese–Native American, and the Manidoo Envoy, who was a friend of Ronin's father, Orion Browne or Nightbreaker, whom Ronin never knew. The narrators meet when Ronin arrives at the Manidoo Hotel in Arizona, searching for his father who had died a week earlier. Ronin then stays to learn what he can of his father and to create memories with the Manidoo Envoy. Each voice is distinguished typographically, with Ronin's text set to look like the novel proper and the Manidoo Envoy's set to look like a typewritten manuscript. The use of two narrative voices, Vizenor explains, is "a way to avoid third person omniscience, which is a giant false voice. [Ronin] . . . is not speaking to a reader. He's speaking a kind of poem, and the dialogue is without direction or notation, you just have to hear it as it goes. . . . That's also the style of kabuki, so I've borrowed this literary sentiment and practice in kabuki."[47] Ronin's chapters are stylized and highly imagistic; each is titled "Ronin of . . ." The Manidoo Envoy's narratives, however, primarily offer explanation, explication, context, and commentary on Ronin's narratives. For example,

Ronin tells how he ironically signs the name "Paul Tibbets" on the T-shirts purchased by tourists at the Peace Memorial Museum. Some seven pages later the Manidoo Envoy explains, "Colonel Paul Tibbets was the pilot of the *Enola Gay*, the plane that released Little Boy, the first atomic bomb, over Hiroshima" (24). In the Manidoo Hotel, Ronin became a storier like his father, one of the several wounded veterans living in the hotel who would choose one of their group as storier for the day. So Ronin's narratives begin as oral stories, transformed into written texts, as the Manidoo Envoy explains: "Ronin became a storier, and he mailed his journal to me several years later with vague instructions to provide notes, the necessary descriptive references, and background information on his father and others. The original stories were first scrawled on scraps of paper and later handwritten in seven ledger notebooks."[48] Other storiers elaborated on Ronin's narrative as it was read aloud at dinner in the hotel, creating a communal story.

Ronin's stories concern the hypocrisy of the concept of "nuclear peace." Together with the graphic scenes of postnuclear devastation and suffering, the deconstruction of the illusion of peace renders Vizenor's novel truly shocking. Ronin writes that "the idea of peace is untrue by nature, a common counterfeit of nations, but the most treacherous peace is based on nuclear victimry" (16). To understand the grounds for Vizenor's scathing critique of the illusion of peace we must return once more to Naanabozho's encounter with the evil Gambler, which, as Proude Cedarfair's encounter reveals, does not destroy evil absolutely and for all time but restores a balance between good and evil. The refusal to permit some nations (such as Japan) to possess nuclear weapons while other nations dominate global politics through nuclear might is exposed by Ronin as dangerous hypocrisy that serves neoimperialist interests. Supplementing this vision, Vizenor presents the discourse of peace as a simulation that is marketed as a commodity in venues such as the Peace Memorial Museum, which Ronin denounces as "a cynical theme park of human misery," "a pathetic romance, a precious token to honor the state memory of a culpable emperor . . . with a sensuous, passive, origami pose of occupational victimry" (18), and the Atomic Bomb Dome, which he calls "a registered haven of cultural shame" (12). As Ronin presents them, these memorials transform peace into its own referent, bearing no relation to a living original, and keep alive a sense of victimry rather than survivance. In the opening chapter he tells how when he first came to live at the Atomic Bomb Dome he was plagued with nightmares, imagining that his "remains were displayed in a diorama of victimry to promote peace" (3).

In a lecture delivered at Keio University in Tokyo in 2004, Vizenor describes Ronin's invisible tattoos as "marks of singularity": "Atomu One on his chest is a remembrance of the ghosts of *atomu* children, as invisible as the tattoos, and to honor *hibakusha* survivance."[49] The children of Hiroshima are at the center of this narrative, not only those who suffered nuclear death but also those who survived. Outside the Atomic Bomb Dome, every morning at the exact moment of the bomb's detonation on August 6, 1945, a "ghost parade" of the dead "children of incineration" protest the "empire war" that killed them (2). Among the children who survived the nuclear bombing are those, like Ronin, who are crossblood or *hafu*. Vizenor addresses the dispossessed status of these children as a result of the Japanese government's refusal to recognize the mixed-blood children who were born during the military occupation of Japan and the restrictive immigration laws in the United States that prevented children finding their American fathers. Ronin finally is adopted by the tribal government of the White Earth Reservation, though he remains a citizen of his birthplace, Japan, and in the last of the Manidoo Envoy's narratives we learn that he ties a T-shirt banner to the waterfront statue of Lafcadio Hearne, the mixed-blood native teacher who became a citizen of Japan. On the banner he has added the word *hafu* to the kamikaze metaphor for duty so that it reads, "I am a glorious *hafu* cherry blossom" (206).

Ronin's *hafu* status links him to both Japanese and to Anishinaabe history. The nuclear devastation of Hiroshima, the novel suggests, is comparable to the invisible holocaust that has decimated tribal communities over the centuries since 1492. *Father Meme* (2008), Vizenor's most recent novel, is dedicated to Dane White and addresses directly the issue of European cultural assaults on tribal communities. In this darkly comic and satirical novel, Vizenor's subversive humor turns to the sensitive and timely subject of child sexual abuse by reservation priests. This subject has been missing from his earlier work on the continuing U.S. genocide against native communities, the cultural devastation experienced by native peoples in the wake of colonization and cultural assimilation, and the survivance of tribal endurance and survival. Vizenor has written in many places about federal boarding schools and other assimilative institutions directed at tribal youth; in this novel his penetrating ironic gaze is focused upon the corrupt and predatory assimilationist mission of Catholic priests on tribal reservations. The novel uses Vizenor's mastery of postmodern narrative technique, but it is firmly grounded in the tribal trickster form that Vizenor has made his very own. This novel shocks and illuminates in equal measure.

Father Meme is a hilarious, heartbreaking satirical trickster tale. The narrative is framed by the encounter in a reservation casino between the debonair unnamed narrator and a French woman tourist, a lawyer on vacation. Over a series of dinners, not unlike the meals shared by Ronin and the Manidoo Envoy in *Hiroshima Bugi*, the narrator develops his story. The narrator is a survivor of, and witness to, the abusive career of the corrupt and evil Roman Catholic priest, the eponymous Father Meme. In a series of scandalous encounters, called the Fourteen Torments and based on the Stations of the Cross, the corrupt priest is challenged and defeated by the power of tribal imagination. Together with his friends, the other altar boys nicknamed Pants and Bear, the trickster-narrator punishes and finally destroys the mythical evil Gambler or symbolic *wiindigoo*. Vizenor's views on such extraliterary issues as tribal casinos, the commodification of native identities and cultures, the lasting impact of U.S. imperialism on tribal lives, and the militants of the American Indian Movement are introduced as part of the framing narrative. The narrator initially translates the native names of menu items for the French tourist, and he goes on to translate for the reader the Anishinaabe terms of the narrative's primary conflict between the tribal boys and the priest, who takes on the metaphysical and mythical dimensions of the evil, monstrous, cannibalistic *wiindigoo* figure of traditional Anishinaabe stories.

The outcome of this conflict is revealed early in the narrative. In the opening pages of the first chapter, the narrator indicts the church as a collaborator with the state in the destructive activities of the fur trade, declaring that "church missions were wicked conspirators in the separation, dominance, and animal genocide."[50] He then goes on to summarize his youthful experience of the wicked Father Meme: the advice of his mother and tribal elders, who do not comprehend the true nature of the abuse, to respect the mission and its priests and to forgive the abusive actions of others; Father Meme's abuse of altar boys and tribal ancestors; and the ultimate sacrifice of the evil priest. As a consequence, suspense is destroyed. But in place of the question "What will happen?" readers are skillfully led to ask, "Why did this happen and how?" In this way the satirical force of the narrative is unleashed from the opening scenes.

Father Meme marks a stylistic departure from Vizenor's earlier fictions, such as *The Trickster of Liberty* (1988), *Griever* (1990), *Dead Voices* (1992), and *Chancers* (2000), characterized as it is by the kind of technical, narratological innovation we find in *Bearheart* and *Hiroshima Bugi*. The humor of this novel supports a scathing indictment of missionary efforts on reservations, where abused adults (parents and elders) cannot perceive the abuse suffered by their children. The generational trauma experienced in a community under colonialist assault by a perverted judicial system and corrupt church is expressed through the sacred "teases" to which the altar boys subject the priest, as they use the sacrificial symbolism of Christianity to persecute him in the righteous cause of tribal survivance. As in all of Vizenor's work, native suffering is set in the context of "survivance," tribal survival and resistance and the refusal of the position of passive victim. In this context it is the reader's laughter at the expense of the abusive priest that works the satire, condemns the evil abuser, and offers salvation of a kind to the survivors. It is Vizenor's extraordinary skill as a satirist that sets this work apart.

The plot is deliberately shaped so that the predatory priest is unable to reduce his young victims to simple prey. Rather, they conspire against him and, using their native wit and intelligence, out-persecute their persecutor. In each of the Fourteen Torments the boys make Father Meme share their terror and horror. Finally the boys kill the priest by beating him to death with lilac sticks and pushing his body into the ice hole where, being sexually aroused by the icy cold, he had so often masturbated. Vizenor tells John Purdy how as a boy he used to make slingshots out of lilac sticks: "It's got a good spring to it."[51] The process by which the narrator tells his story to the French stranger, a vacationing lawyer, transforms the narration into a work of testimony, a remembrance that honors and vindicates all the victims of missionary corruption and genocidal cultural imperialism. But these victims do not succumb to victimry; in this community several priests disappear and no authority will pursue the disappearances. This motif is reminiscent of the disappearing university administrators in Vizenor's novel *Chancers*. The priest's confessional, where he sexually abuses tribal altar boys, is supplanted by the novel-as-confessional, in which a true story ultimately can be told.

The novel is carefully crafted and the language chosen with masterly precision. The narrative is characterized by a sustained set of imagistic oppositions—food as poisonous colonial commodities versus pure tribal nourishment, language in the opposed forms of a corrupting English versus Anishinaabemowin, cold and warmth, presence and absence, good and evil, summer versus winter, icy lake and verdant forest—oppositions that support and develop the satirical uncovering of a world where that which appears to be good and just and holy is in actuality corrupt, hypocritical, and evil.

Throughout his work in the diverse literary genres of poetry, drama, fiction, the essay, history, journalism, and autobiography Vizenor has innovated both in technical and substantive terms. He explores the many strategies by which the category of the "Indian" was invented by whites as cultural genocide, intended to separate tribal people from their heritage and traditions. He acknowledges that the native response was to invent new pan-Indian customs and values and argues that in the process both they and Europeans were blinded to their true cultural heritages. Vizenor's writings expose the simulation, the pretense, and artifice that is the world of invented pan-Indianness and encourage a return to traditional tribal values. The guides for such a return journey are the tricksters and shamans, who still possess the visions, dreams, and myths around which Vizenor's work is woven. Like Naanabozho's wanderings, Vizenor's work is located in "mythic time and transformational space between tribal experiences and dreams."[52] From this place Vizenor enriches our conceptual vocabulary, challenges our familiar ways of understanding the world, and extends the limits of what is possible in contemporary American literature.

Notes

Chapter 1—Overview

1. Louis Owens, "Introduction," *Studies in American Indian Literatures*, 2nd ser., 9 (Spring 1997): 1.

2. John Purdy and Blake Hausman, "The Future of Print Narratives and Comic Holotropes: An Interview with Gerald Vizenor," *American Indian Quarterly* 29 (Winter/Spring 2005): 213.

3. Ibid.

4. Gerald Vizenor and A. Robert Lee, *Postindian Conversations* (Lincoln: University of Nebraska Press, 1999), 27.

5. Ibid., 23.

6. Laura Coltelli, "Gerald Vizenor: The Trickster Heir of Columbus: An Interview," *Native American Literatures Forum* 2–3 (1990–91): 110.

7. Ibid., 111.

8. Vizenor and Lee, *Postindian Conversations*, 59.

9. Ibid., 58.

10. Gerald Vizenor, "Crows Written on the Poplars: Autocritical Autobiographies," in *I Tell You Now: Autobiographical Essays by Native American Writers*, ed. Brian Swann and Arnold Krupat (Lincoln: University of Nebraska Press, 1987), 101.

11. Vizenor and Lee, *Postindian Conversations*, 58.

12. Ibid., 2, 31.

13. Neal Bowers and Charles L. P. Silet, "An Interview with Gerald Vizenor," *MELUS* 8 (Spring 1981): 41.

14. Vizenor and Lee, *Postindian Conversations*, 36–37.

15. Gerald Vizenor, interview with the author, Albuquerque, N.M., October 16, 2008.

16. Gerald Vizenor, interview with the author, Geneva, Switzerland, June 3, 2008.

17. Bowers and Silet, "Interview with Gerald Vizenor," 47.

18. Kenneth Lincoln, *Native American Renaissance* (Berkeley and Los Angeles: University of California Press, 1983).

19. Coltelli, "Gerald Vizenor," 105.

20. Gerald Vizenor, *The Everlasting Sky: New Voices from the People Named the Chippewa* (New York: Collier Macmillan, 1972), 69.

21. Coltelli, "Gerald Vizenor," 106.

22. Purdy and Hausman, "Future of Print Narratives," 217.

23. Robert Silberman, "Gerald Vizenor and *Harold of Orange*: From Word Cinemas to Real Cinema," *American Indian Quarterly* 9 (Winter 1985): 14.

24. Alan Velie, *Four American Indian Literary Masters* (Norman: University of Oklahoma Press, 1982), 144.

25. Coltelli, "Gerald Vizenor," 106.

26. Ibid., 107.

27. Bowers and Silet, "Interview with Gerald Vizenor," 41–42.

28. Hartwig Isernhagen, *Momaday, Vizenor, Armstrong: Conversations on American Indian Writing* (Norman: University of Oklahoma Press, 1999), 98.

29. Ibid., 88.

30. Vizenor and Lee, *Postindian Conversations,* 60.

31. Velie, *Four American Indian Literary Masters,* 135.

32. Ibid., 135–36.

33. Larry McCaffery and Tom Marshall, "Head Water: An Interview with Gerald Vizenor," *Chicago Review* 39, nos. 3–4 (1993): 54.

34. Coltelli, "Gerald Vizenor," 113.

35. Ibid., 114.

36. Isernhagen, *Momaday, Vizenor, Armstrong,* 111.

37. Ibid., 112.

38. Coltelli, "Gerald Vizenor," 102–3.

39. Gerald Vizenor, *Earthdivers: Tribal Narratives on Mixed Descent* (Minneapolis: University of Minnesota Press, 1981), ix.

40. Ibid., xi.

41. Coltelli, "Gerald Vizenor," 104.

42. Bowers and Silet, "Interview with Gerald Vizenor," 47.

43. Gerald Vizenor, "Socioacupuncture: Mythic Reversals and the Striptease in Four Scenes," in *Crossbloods: Bone Courts, Bingo, and Other Reports*, by Gerald Vizenor (1976; repr., Minneapolis: University of Minnesota Press, 1990), 83–84.

44. Ibid., 85.

45. Gerald Vizenor, "Native American Indian Identities: Auto-inscriptions and the Cultures of Names," in *Native American Perspectives on Literature and History*, ed. Alan R. Velie (Norman: University of Oklahoma Press, 1995), 117.

46. Gerald Vizenor, "Imagic Presence: Native Pictomyths and Photographs," in *Literary Chance: Essays on Native American Survivance*, by Gerald Vizenor (Valencia: Biblioteca Javier Coy d'estudis nord-americans, 2007), 103.

47. A. Robert Lee, ed., *Loosening the Seams: Interpretations of Gerald Vizenor* (Bowling Green, Ohio: Bowling Green State University Popular Press, 2000), 5.

48. A. LaVonne Brown Ruoff, "Gerald Vizenor: Compassionate Trickster," *American Indian Quarterly* 9 (Winter 1985): 67.

49. Jack Foley, "Interview with Gerald Vizenor," *Mythosphere* 1, no. 3 (1999): 310.

50. Bowers and Silet, "Interview with Gerald Vizenor," 45.

51. Foley, "Interview with Gerald Vizenor," 316.

52. Coltelli, "Gerald Vizenor," 104.

53. Ibid., 105.

54. Ibid.

55. Ibid.

56. Ibid.

57. Bowers and Silet, "Interview with Gerald Vizenor," 44.

58. Isernhagen, *Momaday, Vizenor, Armstrong,* 129.

59. Gerald Vizenor, *Fugitive Poses: Native American Indian Scenes of Absence and Presence* (Lincoln: University of Nebraska Press, 1998), 15.

60. Chris Lalonde, "The Ceded Landscape of Gerald Vizenor's Fiction," *Studies in American Indian Literatures*, 2nd ser., 9 (Spring 1997): 25.

61. Gerald Vizenor, "American Revolutions: Transethnic Cultures and Narratives," in *Literary Chance: Essays on Native American Survivance,* by Gerald Vizenor (Valencia: Biblioteca Javier Coy d'estudis nord-americans, 2007), 120.

62. Vizenor interview, June 3, 2008.

63. Gerald Vizenor and Alan R. Velie, introduction to *Native American Perspectives on Literature and History,* ed. Alan R. Velie (Norman: University of Oklahoma Press, 1995), 1.

64. Ruoff, "Gerald Vizenor," 73.

65. Gerald Vizenor, *Manifest Manners: Postindian Warriors of Survivance* (Lincoln: University of Nebraska Press, 1999), 63.

66. Vizenor and Lee, *Postindian Conversations,* 83.

67. Ibid., 82.

68. Vizenor, *Four American Indian Literary Masters,* 132.

69. See, for example, Gerald Vizenor, *The People Named the Chippewa: Narrative Histories* (1984; repr., Minneapolis: University of Minnesota Press, 1995), 3.

70. Coltelli, "Gerald Vizenor," 109.

71. Vizenor, *Manifest Manners,* 68.

72. Vizenor and Lee, *Postindian Conversations,* 60.

73. Ibid., 49.

74. Gerald Vizenor, "Gambling on Sovereignty," *American Indian Quarterly* 16, no. 3 (Spring 1992): 412.

75. Ibid.

76. Ibid., 413.

77. Coltelli, "Gerald Vizenor," 103.

78. Vizenor and Lee, *Postindian Conversations,* 79.

79. Coltelli, "Gerald Vizenor," 112.

80. Ibid.

Chapter 2—Gerald Vizenor as Journalist, Tribal Historian, and Cultural Critic

1. Gerald Vizenor and A. Robert Lee, *Postindian Conversations* (Lincoln: University of Nebraska Press, 1999), 81.

2. Kimberly M. Blaeser, *Gerald Vizenor: Writing in the Oral Tradition* (Norman: University of Oklahoma Press, 1996), 40.

3. Gerald Vizenor, *The Everlasting Sky: New Voices from the People Named the Chippewa* (New York: Collier Macmillan, 1972), 69.

4. Gerald Vizenor, *Summer in the Spring: Anishinaabe Lyric Poems and Stories* (Norman: University of Oklahoma Press, 1993), 138. Page references hereafter are given in the text.

5. Vizenor, *Everlasting Sky*, x. Page references hereafter are given in the text.

6. A. LaVonne Brown Ruoff, "Woodland Word Warrior: An Introduction to the Works of Gerald Vizenor," *MELUS* 13 (Spring/Summer 1986): 19; Gerald Vizenor, *Literary Chance: Essays on Native American Survivance* (Valencia: Biblioteca Javier Coy d'estudis nord-americans, 2007).

7. Hartwig Isernhagen, *Momaday, Vizenor, Armstrong: Conversations on American Indian Writing* (Norman: University of Oklahoma Press, 1999), 109.

8. Ibid., 110.

9. Gerald Vizenor, *Wordarrows: Native States of Literary Sovereignty* (Lincoln: University of Nebraska Press, 2003), viii.

10. Ruoff, "Woodland Word Warrior," 21.

11. Vizenor and Lee, *Postindian Conversations*, 80.

12. Ibid., 46.

13. Gerald Vizenor, *Earthdivers: Tribal Narratives on Mixed Descent* (Minneapolis: University of Minnesota Press, 1981), 37.

14. Ibid., 44.

15. Ibid., 46.

16. Ibid., 4.

17. Ibid., 166; Robert Silberman, "Gerald Vizenor and *Harold of Orange*: From Word Cinemas to Real Cinema," *American Indian Quarterly* 9 (Winter 1985): 21n17.

18. Ruoff, "Woodland Word Warrior," 22.

19. A. LaVonne Brown Ruoff, "Gerald Vizenor: Compassionate Trickster," *American Indian Quarterly* 9 (Winter 1985): 70.

20. Linda Ainsworth, "History and the Imagination: Gerald Vizenor's *The People Named the Chippewa*," *Studies in American Indian Literatures* 9 (Winter 1985): 71.

21. Gerald Vizenor, *The People Named the Chippewa: Narrative Histories* (1984; repr., Minneapolis: University of Minnesota Press, 1995), 27.

22. Vizenor, *Earthdivers*, xv. See the discussion of Vizenor's hostility toward anthropologists in Vizenor and Lee, *Postindian Conversations*, 89.

23. John Purdy and Blake Hausman, "The Future of Print Narratives and Comic Holotropes: An Interview with Gerald Vizenor," *American Indian Quarterly* 29 (Winter/Spring 2005): 216.

24. Ruoff, "Woodland Word Warrior," 20. Ruoff remarks on a similarity between Dennis Banks and the character of Coke De Fountain in *Trickster of Liberty* in the story told by Eternal Flame, a character from *Bearheart* (ibid., 21).

25. Gerald Vizenor, "I Know What You Mean, Erdupps MacChurbbs," in *Growing Up in Minnesota: Ten Writers Remember Their Childhoods*, ed. Chester Anderson (Minneapolis: University of Minnesota Press, 1976), 108.

26. Gerald Vizenor, *Tribal Scenes and Ceremonies* (Minneapolis: Nodin Press, 1976), 54.

27. Silberman, "Gerald Vizenor and *Harold of Orange*," 14.

28. Vizenor, *Tribal Scenes and Ceremonies*, 5.

29. Isernhagen, *Momaday, Vizenor, Armstrong*, 121.

30. Ibid., 122–23.

31. Ibid., 120.

32. Ibid., 121.

33. Juana María Rodríguez, "Viznorian Jurisprudence: Legal Interventions, Narrative Strategies, and the Interpretative Possibilities of Shadows," in *Loosening the Seams: Interpretations of Gerald Vizenor*, ed. A. Robert Lee (Bowling Green, Ohio: Bowling Green State University Popular Press, 2000), 258.

34. Vizenor and Lee, *Postindian Conversations,* 83. See Vizenor's discussion of Russell Means in Vizenor and Lee, *Postindian Conversations,* 87.

35. Ibid., 84.

36. Gerald Vizenor, *Manifest Manners: Postindian Warriors of Survivance* (Lincoln: University of Nebraska Press, 1999), 16–17.

37. Gerald Vizenor, *Fugitive Poses: Native American Indian Scenes of Absence and Presence* (Lincoln: University of Nebraska Press, 1998), 11. Page references hereafter are given in the text.

Chapter 3—Gerald Vizenor as Poet

1. Neal Bowers and Charles L. P. Silet, "An Interview with Gerald Vizenor," *MELUS* 8 (Spring 1981): 48.

2. Kimberly M. Blaeser, *Gerald Vizenor: Writing in the Oral Tradition* (Norman: University of Oklahoma Press, 1996), 111–15, offers a succinct overview of this debate.

3. Ibid., 110.

4. Tom Lynch, "To Honor Impermanence: The Haiku and Other Poems of Gerald Vizenor," in *Loosening the Seams: Interpretations of Gerald Vizenor,* ed. A. Robert Lee (Bowling Green, Ohio: Bowling Green State University Popular Press, 2000), 207.

5. Gerald Vizenor, *Raising the Moon Vines* (Minneapolis: Nodin Press, 1964), n.p. Quotations from this text are indicated hereafter parenthetically by the shortened title *Moon Vines*.

6. Gerald Vizenor, *Cranes Arise: Haiku Scenes* (Minneapolis: Nodin Press, 1999), n.p. This book, like all Vizenor's haiku collections, is not paginated; hereafter quotations from this text are indicated in the text parenthetically by title.

7. Jack Foley, "Interview with Gerald Vizenor," *Mythosphere* 1, no. 3 (1999): 317.

8. Bowers and Silet, "Interview with Gerald Vizenor," 42.

9. Kimberly M. Blaeser, "'Interior Dancers': Transformations of Vizenor's Poetic Vision," *Studies in American Indian Literatures*, 2nd ser., 9 (Spring 1997): 8.

10. Gerald Vizenor and A. Robert Lee, *Postindian Conversations* (Lincoln: University of Nebraska Press, 1999), 67.

11. Ibid.

12. Gerald Vizenor, "Envoy to Haiku," *Chicago Review* 39, nos. 3–4 (1993): 55–62; reprinted in *Shadow Distance: A Gerald Vizenor Reader*, ed. A. Robert Lee (Hanover, N.H.: Wesleyan University Press, 1994), 30.

13. Ibid.

14. Ibid., 31.

15. Blaeser, "Interior Dancers," 3.

16. Ibid., 4.

17. Gerald Vizenor, *Matsushima: Pine Islands* (Minneapolis: Nodin Press, 1984), n.p. In order to identify specific poems in this collection, which is not paginated, I have counted and assigned a number to each poem within the section in which it appears.

18. Lynch discusses this use of calligraphy in his essay "To Honor Impermanence."

19. Blaeser, "Interior Dancers," 8.

20. The poems in *Cranes Arise* are glossed with the place where the writing of the poem was inspired. In this way Vizenor draws on the Japanese tradition of *haibun*, a prose style written in the spirit of haiku and about special places the poet has visited. Vizenor defines the genre of *haibun* and its relation to haiku in his introductions to the volumes *Matsushima* and *Cranes Arise*. Vizenor's poetic style remains haiku in *Cranes Arise*, but he makes clear that the haiku poems have been inspired by specific geographical locations.

21. Lynch, "To Honor Impermanence," 211.

22. Ibid., 212.

23. Vizenor and Lee, *Postindian Conversations*, 68.

24. Gerald Vizenor, *Voices of the Rainbow: Contemporary Poetry By Native Americans*, edited by Kenneth Rosen (New York: Viking Press, 1975; repr., New York: Arcade Publishers, 1993), 35–36; quoted by Ruoff, "Woodland Word Warrior," 14. Note that this

poem is substantially different to that published under the same title in Vizenor's *Almost Ashore* (Cambridge: Salt Publishers, 2006), 67.

25. Lynch, "To Honor Impermanence," 217.

26. Vizenor and Lee, *Postindian Conversations*, 33.

27. Blaeser, *Gerald Vizenor*, 113.

28. Quoted in the introduction to *Raising the Moon Vines*, n.p.

29. Vizenor, "Envoy to Haiku," in *Shadow Distance*, 32.

30. Vizenor, *Almost Ashore*, 43. Page references hereafter are given in the text.

31. Gerald Vizenor, *The Everlasting Sky: New Voices from the People Named the Chippewa* (New York: Collier Macmillan, 1972), 69.

32. Ruoff, "Woodland Word Warrior," 15.

33. Elaine Jahner, "Allies in the Word Wars: Vizenor's Uses of Contemporary Critical Theory," *Studies in American Indian Literatures*, 1st ser., 9 (Spring 1985): 68–69.

34. Ibid., 69.

35. Blaeser, "Interior Dancers," 9.

36. John Purdy and Blake Hausman, "The Future of Print Narratives and Comic Holotropes: An Interview with Gerald Vizenor," *American Indian Quarterly* 29 (Winter/Spring 2005): 221–22.

37. Ibid., 222.

38. Jace Weaver, foreword to *Bear Island: The War at Sugar Point*, by Gerald Vizenor (Minneapolis: University of Minnesota Press, 2006), x. Page references hereafter are given in the text.

39. Gerald Vizenor, *Fugitive Poses: Native American Indian Scenes of Absence and Presence* (Lincoln: University of Nebraska Press, 1998), 15.

40. Vizenor, "Imagic Presence." This essay originally appeared as the foreword to Bruce White's book *We Are at Home: Pictures of the Ojibway People* (Minneapolis: Minnesota Historical Society, 2006).

41. Vizenor, "Imagic Presence," 108. Elsewhere, Vizenor describes this necklace as "the traces of liberty" in "Civil War at Sugar Point: The Pillagers of Bear Island," originally presented to the Western

Literature Association, Los Angeles, October 2005. Reprinted in *Literary Chance*, 93.

Chapter 4—Gerald Vizenor as Dramatist

1. Gerald Vizenor, "Reservation Café: The Origin of American Indian Instant Coffee," in *Earth Power Coming*, ed. Simon J. Ortiz (Tsaile, Ariz.: Navajo Community College Press, 1983), 31–36, reprinted in Gerald Vizenor, *Landfill Meditation: Crossblood Stories* (Hanover, N.H.: Wesleyan University Press, 1991), 155–61. Robert Silberman notes this link between the two texts in his "Gerald Vizenor and *Harold of Orange*: From Word Cinemas to Real Cinema," *American Indian Quarterly* 9 (Winter 1985): 18n4.

2. Silberman, "Gerald Vizenor and *Harold of Orange*," 5.

3. Ibid.

4. Gerald Vizenor, *Harold of Orange*, in *Shadow Distance: A Gerald Vizenor Reader*, ed. A. Robert Lee (Hanover, N.H.: Wesleyan University Press & University Press of New England, 1994), 297.

5. Gerald Vizenor, *Harold of Orange*, film (1984, 35 mins.), dir. Richard Weise, prod. Film in the Cities, dist. VisionMaker Video, 1800 N. Thirty-third St., Lincoln, Nebr. 68503. See http://www.visionmaker.org/harold_h.html (accessed August 8, 2008).

6. Gerald Vizenor, "*Harold of Orange*: A Screenplay," *Studies in American Indian Literatures* 5 (Fall 1993): 53.

7. Kimberly M. Blaeser, *Gerald Vizenor: Writing in the Oral Tradition* (Norman: University of Oklahoma Press, 1996), 148.

8. Silberman, "Gerald Vizenor and *Harold of Orange*," 6.

9. Vizenor, *Harold of Orange*, in *Shadow Distance*, 304. Page references hereafter are to this edition and are given in the text.

10. Jack Foley, "Interview with Gerald Vizenor," *Mythosphere* 1, no. 3 (1999): 317.

11. Laura Coltelli, "Gerald Vizenor: The Trickster Heir of Columbus: An Interview," *Native American Literatures Forum* 2–3 (1990–91): 108.

12. Ibid.

13. Karl Kroeber, "Introduction," *Studies in American Indian Literatures*, 1st ser., 9 (Spring 1985): 49.

14. Ibid.

15. Vizenor, "*Harold of Orange:* A Screenplay," 54.

16. Silberman, "Gerald Vizenor and *Harold of Orange,*" 12.

17. James Ruppert, "'Imagination Is the Only Reality. All the Rest Is Bad Television': *Harold of Orange* and Indexical Representation," in *Loosening the Seams: Interpretations of Gerald Vizenor,* ed. A. Robert Lee (Bowling Green, Ohio: Bowling Green State University Popular Press, 2000), 226.

18. Silberman, "Gerald Vizenor and *Harold of Orange,*" 6.

19. Flavia Carriera, "Vizenor's *Harold of Orange,*" *Explicator* 61 (Summer 2003): 240–42.

20. Blaeser, *Gerald Vizenor*, 150.

21. Juana María Rodríguez, "Viznorian Jurisprudence: Legal Interventions, Narrative Strategies, and the Interpretative Possibilities of Shadows," in *Loosening the Seams: Interpretations of Gerald Vizenor,* ed. A. Robert Lee (Bowling Green, Ohio: Bowling Green State University Popular Press, 2000), 250.

22. Gerald Vizenor, "Ishi Obscura," in *Manifest Manners: Postindian Warriors of Survivance* (Lincoln: University of Nebraska Press, 1999), 126.

23. Ibid., 133.

24. Ibid., 127.

25. Ibid., 128.

26. Louis Owens, "The Last Man of the Stone Age: Gerald Vizenor's *Ishi and the Wood Ducks,*" in *Loosening the Seams: Interpretations of Gerald Vizenor,* ed. A. Robert Lee (Bowling Green, Ohio: Bowling Green State University Popular Press, 2000), 233.

27. Gerald Vizenor and A. Robert Lee, *Postindian Conversations* (Lincoln: University of Nebraska Press, 1999), 73.

28. Quoted in Owens, "Last Man of the Stone Age," 234.

29. Quoted in ibid., 236.

30. Quoted in ibid., 237.

31. Gerald Vizenor, *Ishi and the Wood Ducks: Postindian Trickster Comedies,* in *Native American Literature: A Brief Introduction and Anthology,* ed. Gerald Vizenor (New York: HarperCollins, 1995), 301. Page references hereafter are given in the text.

32. Vizenor, *Manifest Manners,* 11.

33. Foley, "Interview with Gerald Vizenor," 312.

34. Elvira Pulitano, "Waiting for Ishi: Gerald Vizenor's *Ishi and the Wood Ducks* and Samuel Beckett's *Waiting for Godot,*" *Studies in American Indian Literatures,* 2nd ser., 9 (Spring 1997): 83.

35. Vizenor, *Manifest Manners,* 127.

36. Vizenor and Lee, *Postindian Conversations,* 73.

37. Pulitano, "Waiting for Ishi," 81.

38. Owens, "Last Man of the Stone Age," 16.

Chapter 5—Gerald Vizenor as Novelist and Storier

1. Diane Glancy, review of *Hotline Healers,* by Gerald Vizenor, *Studies in American Indian Literatures,* 2nd ser., 10 (Summer 1998): 123.

2. Gerald Vizenor, "Native Chance: Clement Vizenor and the Great Depression," in *Literary Chance: Essays on Native American Survivance* (Valencia: Biblioteca Javier Coy d'estudis nord-americans, 2007) 17.

3. Gerald Vizenor, *Landfill Meditation: Crossblood Stories* (Hanover, N.H.: Wesleyan University Press, 1991), 101.

4. John Purdy and Blake Hausman, "The Future of Print Narratives and Comic Holotropes: An Interview with Gerald Vizenor," *American Indian Quarterly* 29 (Winter/Spring 2005): 222.

5. Vizenor, *Landfill Meditation,* 183.

6. Gerald Vizenor and A. Robert Lee, *Postindian Conversations* (Lincoln: University of Nebraska Press, 1999), 69.

7. Gerald Vizenor, *Bearheart: The Heirship Chronicles* (Minneapolis: University of Minnesota Press, 1990), 5, first published as *Darkness in Saint Louis Bearheart* (1978). Elizabeth Blair provides an excellent short account of differences between the two editions of

the novel in "Text as Trickster: Postmodern Language Games in Gerald Vizenor's *Bearheart*," *MELUS* 20 (Winter 1995): 75–90.

8. Gerald Vizenor, *Fugitive Poses: Native American Indian Scenes of Absence and Presence* (Lincoln: University of Nebraska Press, 1998), 6–8.

9. Louis Owens, afterword, in Vizenor, *Bearheart*, 247.

10. Vizenor, *Fugitive Poses*, 7.

11. Ibid.

12. Bernadette Rigel-Cellard, "Doubling in Gerald Vizenor's *Bearheart*: The Pilgrimage Strategy or Bunyan Revisited," *Studies in American Indian Literatures*, 2nd ser., 9 (Spring 1997): 93–94.

13. A. LaVonne Brown Ruoff, "Gerald Vizenor: Compassionate Trickster," *American Indian Quarterly* 9 (Winter 1985): 71.

14. Ibid.

15. Alan R. Velie, "Gerald Vizenor's Indian Gothic," *MELUS* 17 (Spring 1991): 75.

16. Jon Hauss, "Real Stories: Memory, Violence, and Enjoyment in Gerald Vizenor's *Bearheart*," *Literature and Psychology* 41 (1995): 2.

17. Vizenor, *Bearheart*, vii. Page references hereafter are given in the text.

18. Rigel-Cellard, "Doubling in Gerald Vizenor's *Bearheart*," 102.

19. Nora Baker Barry, "Postmodern Bears in the Texts of Gerald Vizenor," *MELUS* 27 (Fall 2002): 93.

20. Ibid., 101.

21. Ibid.

22. Velie, "Gerald Vizenor's Indian Gothic," 75–76.

23. Rigel-Cellard, "Doubling in Gerald Vizenor's *Bearheart*," 97.

24. Ibid., 109.

25. Bradley John Monsma, "Liminal Landscapes: Motion, Perspective, and Place in Gerald Vizenor's Fiction," *Studies in American Indian Literatures*, 2nd ser., 9 (Spring 1997): 62.

26. Ibid., 63.

27. Vizenor and Lee, *Postindian Conversations*, 54.

28. Linda Lizut Helstern, "Blue Smoke and Mirrors: Griever's Buddhist Heart," *Studies in American Indian Literatures*, 2nd ser., 9 (Spring 1997): 33.

29. Linda Lizut Helstern, "*Griever: An American Monkey King in China*: A Cross-Cultural Re-membering," in *Loosening the Seams: Interpretations of Gerald Vizenor*, ed. A. Robert Lee (Bowling Green, Ohio: Bowling Green State University Popular Press, 2000), 136–54.

30. Ibid., 136.

31. Gerald Vizenor, *Dead Voices* (Norman: University of Oklahoma Press, 1992), 17.

32. Gerald Vizenor, "Authored Animals: Creature Tropes in Native American Fiction," *Social Research* 62, no. 3 (1995): 661–83; available online at http://findarticles.com/p/articles/mi_m2267/is_n3_v62/ai_17909886 (accessed May 24, 2007).

33. Ibid.

34. Ibid.

35. Ibid.

36. Gerald Vizenor, *Hotline Healers: An Almost Browne Novel* (Hanover, N.H.: Wesleyan University Press, 1997), 2.

37. Helstern, "*Griever*," 148.

38. Gerald Vizenor, *Griever: An American Monkey King in China* (Minneapolis: University of Minnesota Press, 1990), 225. Page preferences hereafter are given in the text.

39. Helstern, "*Griever*," 150.

40. Ibid., 140.

41. Gerald Vizenor, *The Trickster of Liberty: Native Heirs to a Wild Baronage* (Norman: University of Oklahoma Press, 1988), 131.

42. Helstern, "Blue Smoke and Mirrors," 38.

43. Ibid.

44. Helstern, "*Griever*," 151–52.

45. Ibid., 151.

46. Neal Bowers and Charles L. P. Silet, "An Interview with Gerald Vizenor," *MELUS* 8 (Spring 1981): 43.

47. Purdy and Hausman, "Future of Print Narratives," 221.

48. Gerald Vizenor, *Hiroshima Bugi: Atomu 57* (Lincoln: University of Nebraska Press, 2003), 9. Page references hereafter are given in the text.

49. Gerald Vizenor, "Ishmael Ashore in Hiroshima: Moby Dick, Ranald MacDonald, and Ronin Browne," in Vizenor, *Literary Chance,* 113.

50. Gerald Vizenor, *Father Meme* (Albuquerque: University of New Mexico Press, 2008), 5. Page references hereafter will be given in the text.

51. Purdy and Hausman, "Future of Print Narratives," 222.

52. Gerald Vizenor, *The People Named the Chippewa: Narrative Histories* (1984; repr., Minneapolis: University of Minnesota Press, 1995), 3.

Bibliography

Works by Gerald Vizenor

Almost Ashore. Cambridge, U.K.: Salt Publishers, 2006.

"Almost a Whole Trickster." In *A Gathering of Flowers,* edited by Joyce Carol Thomas, 1–20. New York: Harper & Row, 1990.

"Almost Browne." *Indian Youth of America Newsletter*, Winter 1988.

"The Animosh Driving School." *Stand Magazine* 8, no. 1 (Leeds University, England), Fall 2007, 7–10.

Anishinabe adisokan: Tales of the People. Minneapolis: Nodin, 1970.

Anishinabe nagamon: Songs of the People. Minneapolis: Nodin, 1970.

"Authored Animals: Creature Tropes in Native American Fiction." *Social Research* 62 (Fall 1995): 661–83. Available online at http://findarticles.com/p/articles/mi_m2267/is_n3_v62/ai_17909886 (accessed May 24, 2007). Reprinted in *Humans and Other Animals*, edited by Arien Mack, 249–72. Columbus: Ohio State University Press, 1999.

"Bad Breath." In *An Illuminated History of the Future,* edited by Curtis White, 135–64. Normal: Illinois State University and Fiction Collective Two, 1989.

Bearheart: The Heirship Chronicles. Minneapolis: University of Minnesota Press, 1990. First published as *Darkness in Saint Louis Bearheart*. St. Paul, Minn.: Truck Press, 1978.

Bear Island: The War at Sugar Point. Minneapolis: University of Minnesota Press, 2006.

"Bone Courts: The Natural Rights of Tribal Remains." In *The Interrupted Life,* 55–67. New York: Museum of Contemporary Art, 1991.

"Bone Courts: The Rights and Narrative Representations of Tribal Bones." *American Indian Quarterly* 10 (Autumn 1986): 319–31.

Reprinted in *Contemporary Archaeology in Theory*, edited by Robert Preucel and Ian Hodder, 652–64. Oxford: Blackwell, 1996.

"Bound Feet." *Fiction International* 17 (Spring 1987): 4–8.

"Casino Coups." In *Culture and the Imagination: Proceedings of the Third Stuttgart Seminar on Cultural Studies*, edited by Heide Ziegler, 107–16. Stuttgart: Verlag Für Wissenschaft und Forschung, 1995.

Chancers. Norman: University of Oklahoma Press, 2000. French translation: *Crâneurs*. Translated by Thierry Chevrier. Paris: Éditions du Rocher, 2007.

"Christopher Columbus: Lost Havens in the Ruins of Representation." *American Indian Quarterly* 16 (Fall 1992): 521–32.

"Confrontation or Negotiation." In *Native American Testimony: A Chronicle of Indian-White Relations from Prophecy to Present, 1492–1992*, edited by Peter Nabokov, 377–80. New York: Viking Penguin, 1991.

Cranes Arise: Haiku Scenes. Minneapolis: Nodin Press, 1999.

Crossbloods: Bone Courts, Bingo, and Other Reports. Minneapolis: University of Minnesota Press, 1990.

"Crows Written on the Poplars: Autocritical Autobiographies." In *I Tell You Now: Autobiographical Essays by Native American Writers*, edited by Brian Swann and Arnold Krupat, 99–109. Lincoln: University of Nebraska Press, 1987. Reprinted in *Native American Autobiography*, edited by Arnold Krupat, 425–34. Madison: University of Wisconsin Press, 1994.

Darkness in Saint Louis Bearheart. St. Paul, Minn.: Truck Press, 1978. Revised edition published as *Bearheart: The Heirship Chronicles*. Minneapolis: University of Minnesota Press, 1990.

Dead Voices: Natural Agonies in the New World. Norman: University of Oklahoma Press, 1992.

Earthdivers: Tribal Narratives on Mixed Descent. Minneapolis: University of Minnesota Press, 1981.

"Edward Curtis: Pictorialist and Ethnographic Adventurist." In *Edward S. Curtis's "The North American Indian."* National

Digital Library Program. Library of Congress, 2001. Reprinted in *True West*, edited by William R. Handley and Nathaniel Lewis, 179–93. Lincoln: University of Nebraska Press, 2004.

"The Elevator Shaman." In *XCP: Cross Cultural Poetics* 4 (April 1999): 84–92.

Empty Swings. Minneapolis: Nodin Press, 1967.

"The Envoy to Haiku." *Chicago Review* 39, nos. 3–4 (1993): 55–62.

"Episodes in Mythic Verism: Monsignor Missalwait's Interstate." In *The New Native American Novel: Works in Progress*, edited by Mary Dougherty, 109–26. Albuquerque: University of New Mexico Press, 1986.

"Ethnic Derivatives." In *Stories Migrating Home: A Collection of Anishinaabe Prose*, edited by Kimberly Blaeser, 194–206. Bemidji, Minn.: Loonfeather Press, 1999.

The Everlasting Sky: New Voices from the People Named the Chippewa. New York: Collier Macmillan, 1972. Reprinted with new introduction as *The Everlasting Sky: Voices of the Anishinabe People*. St. Paul: Minnesota Historical Society Press, 2001.

Father Meme. Albuquerque: University of New Mexico Press, 2008.

"Feral Lasers." *Caliban* 6 (Fall 1989): 16–23.

"Four Skin." *Tamaqua* 2 (Winter 1991): 89–104.

"Fugitive Poses." In *Excavating Voices: Listening to Photographs of Native Americans*, edited by Michael Katakis, 7–16. Philadelphia: University of Pennsylvania Museum, 1998.

Fugitive Poses: Native American Indian Scenes of Absence and Presence. Abraham Lincoln Lecture Series. Lincoln: University of Nebraska Press, 1998. Japanese translation, 2003.

"Fusions of Survivance: Haiku Scenes and Native Dream Songs." *Modern Haiku* 31, no. 1 (2000): 37–47.

"Gambling." In *Encyclopedia of North American Indians*, edited by Frederick Hoxie, 212–14. New York: Houghton Mifflin, 1996.

"Gambling on Sovereignty." *American Indian Quarterly* 16 (Spring 1992): 411–13.

"George Morrison: Anishinaabe Expressionism at Red Rock." In *National Museum of American Indian Art*. Inaugural exhibition catalogue essay. Washington, D.C.: Smithsonian Institution, 2004.

"George Morrison: Anishinaabe Expressionist Artist." *American Indian Quarterly* 30 (Fall 2006): 646–60.

"Gerald Vizenor." *Zyzzyva* (Winter 1992). Reprinted in *The Writer's Notebook*, edited by Howard Junker, 219–34. New York: HarperCollins, 1995.

"Gerald Vizenor: Visions, Scares, and Stories." In *Contemporary Authors,* 255–77. Contemporary Authors Autobiography Series 22. Detroit: Gale Research, 1995.

Griever: An American Monkey King in China. New York: Fiction Collective, 1987. Reprint, Minneapolis: University of Minnesota Press, 1990.

Harold of Orange. In *Shadow Distance: A Gerald Vizenor Reader*, edited by A. Robert Lee, 297–333. Hanover, N.H.: Wesleyan University Press & University Press of New England, 1994.

"*Harold of Orange:* A Screenplay." *Studies in American Indian Literatures* 5 (Fall 1993): 53–88.

Harold of Orange / Harold von Orangen. Bilingual edition of *Harold of Orange: A Screenplay.* Translated by Wolfgang Hochbruck et al. Eddingen: Osnabrück, 1994.

The Heirs of Columbus. Hanover, N.H.: Wesleyan University Press, 1991.

Hiroshima Bugi: Atomu 57. Lincoln: University of Nebraska Press, 2003.

Hotline Healers: An Almost Browne Novel. Hanover, N.H.: Wesleyan University Press, 1997.

"I Know What You Mean, Erdupps MacChurbbs." In *Growing Up in Minnesota: Ten Writers Remember Their Childhoods*, edited by Chester Anderson, 79–111. Minneapolis: University of Minnesota Press, 1976.

"Imagic Moments: Native Identities and Literary Modernity." *Third Text* 46 (Spring 1999): 25–37. Reprinted in *Imaginary (Re)Locations: Tradition, Modernity, and the Market in Contemporary*

Native American Literature and Culture, edited by Helmbrecht Breinig, 167–84. Tubingen: Stauffenburg Verlag, 2003.

"Indian Identity." In *A Companion to American Thought*, edited by Richard Wightman Fox and James Kloppenberg, 331–33. New York: Blackwell, 1995.

Interior Landscapes: Autobiographical Myths and Metaphors. Minneapolis: University of Minnesota Press, 1990.

"An Introduction to Haiku." *Neeuropa*, Summer 1991/Spring 1992, 63–67.

Ishi and the Wood Ducks. In *Native American Literature: A Brief Introduction and Anthology*, edited by Gerald Vizenor, 299–336. New York: HarperCollins, 1995.

"Ishi Bares His Chest: Tribal Simulations and Survivance." In *Partial Recall: Photographs of Native North Americans*, edited by Lucy Lippard, 65–72. New York: New Press, 1992.

Landfill Meditation: Crossblood Stories. Hanover, N.H.: Wesleyan University Press, 1991.

"The Last Lecture on the Edge." In *American Indian Literature: An Anthology,* edited by Alan R. Velie, 339–47. Norman: University of Oklahoma Press, 1991.

Literary Chance: Essays on Native American Survivance. Valencia: Biblioteca Javier Coy d'estudis nord-americans, 2007.

"Literary Gambling Sticks." *Alaska Quarterly Review* 17, no. 3/4 (1999): xi–xvi.

"Luminous Thighs." In *The Lightning Within: An Anthology of Contemporary American Indian Fiction,* edited by Alan Velie, 67–90. Norman: University of Oklahoma Press, 1991.

"Manifest Manners: The Long Gaze of Christopher Columbus." *boundary 2* 19 (Autumn 1992): 223–35.

Manifest Manners: Postindian Warriors of Survivance. Lincoln: University of Nebraska Press, 1999. First published as *Manifest Manners: Postindian Warriors of Survivance*. Hanover, N.H.: Wesleyan University Press, 1994.

Matsushima: Pine Islands. Minneapolis: Nodin Press, 1984.

"Mercenary Sovereignty: Casinos, Truth Games, and Native American Liberty." In *Cultural Encounters in the New World*, edited by Harald Zapf and Klaus Lösch, 311–324. Tubingen: Gunter Narr Verlag, 2003.

"Mister Ishi: Analogies of Exile, Deliverance, and Liberty." In *Ishi in Three Centuries*, edited by Karl Kroeber, 363–72. Lincoln: University of Nebraska Press, 2003.

"Mister Ishi: A Personal Essay." *California Monthly* 111 (November 2000): 29. Reprinted in *California Magazine*, April 2007, 29ff.

"The Moccasin Game." In *Earth Songs, Sky Spirit*, edited by Clifford Trafzer, 37–62. New York: Doubleday, 1993.

"Moccasin Games." *Caliban* 9 (Spring 1990): 96–109.

"Monte Cassino Curiosa: Heart Dancers at the Headwaters." *Caliban* 14 (1994): 60–70. Reprinted in *Re/mapping the Occident*, edited by Bryan Joachim Malessa and John Jason Mitchell, 69–83. Berkeley and Los Angeles: University of California Press, 1995.

"Naming of Ishi Court." *News from Native California*, Summer 1993, 40–41.

"Narrative Chance." *Before Columbus Review* 1 (Fall–Winter 1989): 9–10.

Editor. *Narrative Chance: Postmodern Discourse on Native American Indian Literatures*. Norman: University of Oklahoma Press, 1989.

"Native American Dissolve." *Oshkaabewis Native Journal* 1, no. 1 (1990): 63–65.

"Native American Indian Identities: Autoinscriptions and the Cultures of Names." *Genre* 24, no. 4 (1994): 431–40. Reprinted in *Native American Perspectives on Literature and History*, edited by Alan R. Velie, 117–26. Norman: University of Oklahoma Press, 1995.

"Native American Indian Literature: Critical Metaphors of the Ghost Dance." *World Literature Today* 66, (Spring 1992): 223–27.

Native American Literature: A Brief Introduction and Anthology. [Editor.] New York: HarperCollins, 1995.

"Native American Narratives: Resistance and Survivance." In *A Companion to American Fiction 1865–1914*, edited by Robert Lamb and G. R. Thompson, 222–39. Oxford: Blackwell, 2005.

Native Liberty: Natural Reason or Cultural Survivance. Lincoln: University of Nebraska Press, 2009.

Native Storiers: Five Selections. [Editor.] Lincoln: University of Nebraska Press, 2009.

"Not 'Chippewa,' Not 'Ojibway' . . . Anishinaabe." In *Ringing in the Wilderness: Selections from the North Country Anvil*, edited by Rhoda R. Gilman, 269–72. Duluth, Minn.: Holy Cow! Press, 1996.

The Old Park Sleeper. Privately printed, 1961. Reprint, Minneapolis: Callimachus, 1961.

"Oshkiwiinag: Heartlines on the Trickster Express." *Religion and Literature* 26 (Spring 1994): 89–106. Reprinted in *The Year's Best Fantasy and Horror*, edited by Ellen Datlow and Terri Windling, 480–94. New York: St. Martin's Press, 1997.

"Oshkiwiinag: Heartlines on the Trickster Express." *Stand Magazine* 8, no. 1 (Leeds University, England), Fall 2007, 10–23.

"Our Land: Anishinaabe." *Native Peoples Magazine*, Spring 1993, 32–35.

The People Named the Chippewa: Narrative Histories. 1984. Reprint, Minneapolis: University of Minnesota Press, 1995.

"The Pink Flamingos." *Caliban* 7 (Winter 1989): 140–49.

"Postindian Autoinscriptions: The Origins of Essentialism and Pluralism in Descriptive Tribal Names." In *Cultural Differences and the Literary Text*, edited by Winfried Siemerling and Katrin Schwenk, 29–39. Iowa City: University of Iowa Press, 1996.

Postindian Conversations. With A. Robert Lee. Lincoln: University of Nebraska Press, 1999.

"Postmodern Discourse on Native American Literature." *Halcyon* 12 (1990): 43–48.

"Prison Riders." In *Native American Voices on Identity, Art, and Culture: Objects of Everlasting Esteem*, edited by Lucy Fowler Williams, William Wierzbowski, and Robert Preucel, 59–60. Philadelphia: University of Pennsylvania, Museum of Archaeology and Anthropology, 2005.

Quasi en Terra. Translated by Carme Manuel Cuenca. Valencia: Editorial Denes Poesia Edicions de la Guerra, 2009.

Raising the Moon Vines. 1964. Reprint, Minneapolis: Nodin Press, 1999.

"Reservation Café: The Origin of American Indian Instant Coffee." In *Earth Power Coming: Short Fiction in Native American Literature,* edited by Simon J. Ortiz, 31–36. Tsaile, Ariz.: Navajo Community College Press, 1983.

"Reversal of Fortunes: Tribalism in the Nick of Time." *Caliban* 13 (1993): 22–28.

"The Ruins of Representation: Shadow Survivance and the Literature of Dominance." In *An Other Tongue*, edited by Alfred Arteaga, 139–68. Durham, N.C.: Duke University Press, 1994.

"Santa Maria Casino." Dramatic script of a one-act play. *Berkeley Fiction Review,* no. 13 (1993): 12–21.

Seventeen Chirps. Minneapolis: Nodin Press, 1968.

Shadow Distance: A Gerald Vizenor Reader. Hanover, N.H.: Wesleyan University Press, 1994.

Slight Abrasions: A Dialogue in Haiku. With Jerome Downes. Minneapolis: Nodin Press, 1966.

"Socioacupuncture: Mythic Reversals and the Striptease in Four Scenes." In *The American Indian and Problems of History,* edited by Calvin Martin, 180–91. New York: Oxford University Press, 1987.

South of the Painted Stones. Minneapolis: Callimachus, 1963.

"The Stone Babies." *Weber Studies* 16, no. 2 (Winter 1999). http://weberstudies.weber.edu/archive/archive%20C%20Vol.%2016.2–18.1/Vol.%2016.2 /geraldvizenor.html (accessed August 7, 2008).

"Stone Columbus: Talk Radio from the Santa Maria Casino." In *After Yesterday's Crash: The Avant-Pop Anthology*, edited by Larry McCaffery, 220–32. New York: Viking Penguin, 1995.

"The Stone Trickster." *Northeast Indian Quarterly* 8 (Fall 1991): 23–31.

Summer in the Spring: Ojibwe Lyric Poems and Tribal Stories. 1970. Reprint, Minneapolis: Nodin Press, 1981. Revised edition: *Summer in the Spring: Anishinaabe Lyric Poems and Stories*. Norman: University of Oklahoma Press, 1993.

Survivance: Narratives of Native Presence. [Editor.] Lincoln: University of Nebraska Press, 2008.

"A Sweeping Tale of Emigration." Review of *In America*, by Susan Sontag. *Minneapolis Star Tribune*, April 2, 2000.

Thomas James White Hawk. Minneapolis: Four Winds Press, 1968.

Touchwood: A Collection of Ojibway Prose. [Editor.] 1987. Reprint, Moorhead, Minn.: New Rivers Press, 1994.

"The Tragic Wisdom of Salamanders." *Caliban* 12 (1993): 16–27. Reprinted in *Sacred Trusts: Essays on Stewardship and Responsibility*, edited by Michael Katakis, 161–76. San Francisco: Mercury House, 1993.

"Transethnic Anthropologism: Comparative Ethnic Studies at Berkeley." *Studies in American Indian Literatures* 7 (Winter 1995): 3–8. Reprinted in *Margins in British and American Literature, Film and Culture*, edited by Marita Nadal and M. Delores Herrero, 181–87. Zaragoza, Spain: Departamento de Filología Inglesa y Alemana, Universidad de Zaragoza, 1997.

Tribal Scenes and Ceremonies. Minneapolis: Nodin Press, 1976.

"Trickster Discourse." *Wicazo Sa Review,* Spring 1989, 2–7.

"Trickster Discourse: Comic and Tragic Themes in Native American Literature." In *Buried Roots and Indestructible Seeds*, edited by Mark A. Lindquist and Martin Zanger, 67–83. Madison: University of Wisconsin Press, 1994.

"Trickster Hermeneutics." In *Reverberations: Tactics of Resistance, Forms of Agency in Trans/Cultural Practices*, edited by Jean Fisher, 142–50. Maastricht: Jan van Eyck Edition, 2000.

The Trickster of Liberty: Tribal Heirs to a Wild Baronage. Minneapolis: University of Minnesota Press, 1988. Reprint, Norman: University of Oklahoma Press, 2005.

"Trickster Photography: Simulations in the Ethnographic Present." *Exposure: Society for Photographic Education*, Fall 1993, 4–5.

Two Wings the Butterfly. Privately printed, 1960.

"Visual Image of Gover's Apology Draws Analogies." Editorial commentary. *Native American Press / Ojibwe News* (St. Paul, Minn.), October 20, 2000.

"Wampum to Pictures of Presidents." In *From Different Shores: Perspectives on Race and Ethnicity in America,* edited by Ronald Takaki, 126–28. New York: Oxford University Press, 1987.

Water Striders. Porter Broadside Series. Santa Cruz, Calif.: Moving Parts Press, 1989.

"Wingo on the Santa Maria." In *Avant-Pop: Fiction for a Daydream Nation,* edited by Larry McCaffery, 199–206. Boulder, Colo.: Black Ice Books, 1993.

Wordarrows: Native States of Literary Sovereignty. Lincoln: University of Nebraska Press, 2003. First published as *Wordarrows: Indians and Whites in the New Fur Trade*. 1978. Reprint, Minneapolis: University of Minnesota Press, 1989. Italian translation: *Parolefrecce*. Translated by Maria Vittoria D'Amico. Pisa: University of Pisa, 1992.

Works about Gerald Vizenor

Ainsworth, Linda. "History and the Imagination: Gerald Vizenor's *The People Named the Chippewa*." *Studies in American Indian Literatures* 9 (Winter 1985): 70–80.

Barry, Nora. "Chance and Ritual: The Gambler in the Texts of Gerald Vizenor." *Studies in American Indian Literatures* 5 (Fall 1993): 13–22.

Barry, Nora Baker. "Postmodern Bears in the Texts of Gerald Vizenor." *MELUS* 27 (Fall 2002): 93–112.

Binder, Wolfgang, and Helmbrecht Breinig. "Gerald Vizenor." In *American Contradictions: Interviews with Nine American Writers,* edited by Wolfgang Binder and Helmbrecht Breinig, 143–65. Hanover, N.H.: Wesleyan University Press, 1995.

Blaeser, Kimberly M. *Gerald Vizenor: Writing in the Oral Tradition*. Norman: University of Oklahoma Press, 1996.

———. "'Interior Dancers': Transformations of Vizenor's Poetic Vision." *Studies in American Indian Literatures*, 2nd ser., 9 (Spring 1997): 3–15.

Blair, Elizabeth. "Text as Trickster: Postmodern Language Games in Gerald Vizenor's Bearheart." *MELUS* 20 (Winter 1995): 75–90.

Bowers, Neal, and Charles L. P. Silet. "An Interview with Gerald Vizenor." *MELUS* 8 (Spring 1981): 41–49.

Boyarin, Jonathan. "Europe's Indian, America's Jew: Modiano and Vizenor." *boundary 2* 19 (Autumn 1992): 197–222. Reprinted in Jonathan Boyarin. *Storm from Paradise: The Politics of Jewish Memory*. Minneapolis: University of Minnesota Press, 1992. Reprinted in *American Indian Persistence and Resurgence*, edited by Karl Kroeber, 198–223. Durham, N.C.: Duke University Press, 1994.

Bruchac, Joseph. "Follow the Trickroutes: An Interview with Gerald Vizenor." In *Survival This Way: Interviews with American Indian Poets*, edited by Joseph Bruchac, 287–310. Tucson: University of Arizona Press, 1987.

Burgess, Benjamin V. "Elaboration Therapy in the Midewiwin and Gerald Vizenor's *The Heirs of Columbus*." *Studies in American Indian Literatures* 18 (Spring 2006): 22–36.

Carriera, Flavia. "Vizenor's *Harold of Orange*." *Explicator* 61 (Summer 2003): 240–42.

Christie, Stuart. "Trickster Gone Golfing: Vizenor's *Heirs of Columbus* and the Chelh-ten-em Development Controversy." *American Indian Quarterly* 21 (Summer 1998): 359–84.

Coltelli, Laura. "Gerald Vizenor: The Trickster Heir of Columbus: An Interview." *Native American Literatures Forum* 2–3 (1990–91): 101–15.

Foley, Jack. "Interview with Gerald Vizenor." *Mythosphere* 1, no. 3 (1999): 304–17.

Gamber, John Blair. "'Outcasts and Dreamers in the Cities': Urbanity and Pollution in *Dead Voices*." *PMLA* 122 (January 2007): 179–93.

Gray, James A. "Mediating Narratives of American Indian Identity." *Contemporary Literature* 39 (Spring 1998): 146–55.

Gross, Lawrence W. "The Comic Vision of Anishinaabe Culture and Religion." *American Indian Quarterly* 26 (Summer 2002): 436–59.

Hardin, Michael. "The Trickster of History: *The Heirs of Columbus* and the Dehistorization of Narrative." *MELUS* 23 (Winter 1998): 25–45.

Haseltine, Patricia. "The Voices of Gerald Vizenor: Survival through Transformation." *American Indian Quarterly* 9 (Winter 1985): 31–47.

Hauss, Jon. "Real Stories: Memory, Violence, and Enjoyment in Gerald Vizenor's *Bearheart*." *Literature & Psychology* 41, no. 4 (1995): 1–17.

Helstern, Linda Lizut. "'Bad Breath': Gerald Vizenor's Lacanian Fable." *Studies in Short Fiction* 36 (Fall 1999): 351–61.

———. "Blue Smoke and Mirrors: Griever's Buddhist Heart." *Studies in American Indian Literatures*, 2nd ser., 9 (Spring 1997): 33–46.

Hochbruck, Wolfgang. "Breaking Away: The Novels of Gerald Vizenor." *World Literature Today* 66 (Spring 1992): 274–79.

Isernhagen, Hartwig. *Momaday, Vizenor, Armstrong: Conversations on American Indian Writing*. Norman: University of Oklahoma Press, 1999.

Jahner, Elaine. "Allies in the Word Wars: Vizenor's Uses of Contemporary Critical Theory." *Studies in American Indian Literatures*, 1st ser., 9 (Spring 1985): 64–70.

Jalalzai, Zubeda. "Tricksters, Captives, and Conjurers: The 'Roots' of Liminality and Gerald Vizenor's *Bearheart*." *American Indian Quarterly* 23 (Winter 1999): 25–44.

Keady, Maureen. "Walking Backward into the Fourth World: Survival of the Fittest in *Bearheart*." *American Indian Quarterly* (Winter 1985): 61–65.

Kroeber, Karl. "Introduction." *Studies in American Indian Literatures*, 1st ser., 9 (Spring 1985): 49–52. Special issue on Gerald Vizenor.

Krupat, Arnold. "Stories in the Blood: Ratio- and Natio- in Gerald Vizenor's *The Heirs of Columbus*." In *Loosening the Seams: Interpretations of Gerald Vizenor*, edited by A. Robert Lee, 166–77. Bowling Green, Ohio: Bowling Green State University Press, 2000.

———. *The Turn to the Native: Studies in Criticism and Culture.* Lincoln: University of Nebraska Press, 1997.

Laga, Barry E. "Gerald Vizenor and His Heirs of Columbus: A Postmodern Quest for More Discourse." *American Indian Quarterly* 18 (Winter 1994): 71–87.

Lalonde, Chris. "The Ceded Landscape of Gerald Vizenor's Fiction." *Studies in American Indian Literatures*, 2nd ser., 9 (Spring 1997): 16–32.

Lee, A. Robert, ed. *Loosening the Seams: Interpretations of Gerald Vizenor.* Bowling Green, Ohio: Bowling Green State University Popular Press, 2000.

Liang, Iping. "Opposition Play: Trans-Atlantic Trickstering in Gerald Vizenor's *The Heirs of Columbus*." *Concentric: Studies in English Literature and Linguistics* 29 (January 2003): 121–41.

Lincoln, Kenneth. *Native American Renaissance.* Berkeley and Los Angeles: University of California Press, 1983.

Linton, Patricia. "The 'Person' in Postmodern Fiction: Gibson, Le Guin, and Vizenor." *Studies in American Indian Literatures* 5 (Fall 1993): 3–11.

Lowe, John. "Monkey Kings and Mojo: Postmodern Ethnic Humor in Kingston, Reed, and Vizenor." *MELUS* 21 (Winter 1996): 103–27.

McCaffery, Larry. "On Thin Ice, You Might as Well Dance." In *Some Other Frequency: Interviews with Innovative American Authors*, by Larry McCaffery, 287–309. Philadelphia: University of Pennsylvania Press, 1996.

McCaffery, Larry, and Tom Marshall. "Head Water: An Interview with Gerald Vizenor." *Chicago Review* 39, nos. 3–4 (1993): 50–54.

Miller, Dallas. "Mythic Rage and Laughter: An Interview with Gerald Vizenor." *Studies in American Indian Literatures* 7 (Spring 1995): 77–96.

Monsma, Bradley John. "Liminal Landscapes: Motion, Perspective, and Place in Gerald Vizenor's Fiction." *Studies in American Indian Literatures*, 2nd ser., 9 (Spring 1997): 60–72.

Murray, David. "Crossblood Strategies in the Writings of Gerald Vizenor." *Yearbook of English Studies* 24 (1994): 213–27.

Owens, Louis. "Ecstatic Strategies: Gerald Vizenor's Trickster Narratives." In *Other Destinies: Understanding the American Indian Novel*, 225–54. Norman: University of Oklahoma Press, 1992.
———. "Introduction." *Studies in American Indian Literatures*, 2nd ser., 9 (Spring 1997): 1–3. Special issue on Gerald Vizenor.

Pearson, Stephen J. "The Monkey King in the American Canon: Patricia Chao and Gerald Vizenor's Use of an Iconic Chinese Character." *Comparative Literature Studies* 43 (2006): 355–74.

Powell, Malea. "Rhetorics of Survivance: How American Indians Use Writing." *College Composition and Communication* 53 (February 2002): 396–434.

Pulitano, Elvira. *Towards a Native American Critical Theory*. Lincoln: University of Nebraska Press, 2002.
———. "Waiting for Ishi: Gerald Vizenor's *Ishi and the Wood Ducks* and Samuel Beckett's *Waiting for Godot*." *Studies in American Indian Literatures*, 2nd ser., 9 (Spring 1997): 73–92.

Purdy, John, and Blake Hausman. "The Future of Print Narratives and Comic Holotropes: A Conversation with Gerard Vizenor." *American Indian Quarterly* 29 (Winter/Spring 2005): 212–25.

Rigel-Cellard, Bernadette. "Doubling in Gerald Vizenor's *Bearheart*: The Pilgrimage Strategy or Bunyan Revisited." *Studies in American Indian Literatures*, 2nd ser., 9 (Spring 1997): 93–114.

Rolo, Mark Anthony. "Gerald Vizenorisms." *Circle: Native American News and Arts* (Minneapolis), 30 June 1997.

Ruoff, A. LaVonne Brown. "Gerald Vizenor: Compassionate Trickster." *Studies in American Indian Literatures*, 1st ser., 9 (Spring 1985): 52–63.

———. "Gerald Vizenor: Compassionate Trickster." *American Indian Quarterly* 9 (Winter 1985): 67–73.

———. "Woodland Word Warrior: An Introduction to the Works of Gerald Vizenor." *MELUS* 13 (Spring/Summer 1986): 13–43.

Ruppert, James. *Mediation in Contemporary Native American Fiction*. Norman: University of Oklahoma Press, 1995.

Schmidt, Kerstin. "Subverting the Dominant Paradigm: Gerald Vizenor's Trickster Discourse." *Studies in American Indian Literatures* 7 (Spring 1995): 65–76.

Schweninger, Lee. "Claiming Europe: Native American Literary Responses to the Old World." *American Indian Culture & Research Journal* 27 (2003): 61–76.

Silberman, Robert. "Gerald Vizenor and *Harold of Orange*: From Word Cinemas to Real Cinema." *American Indian Quarterly* 9 (Winter 1985): 5–21.

Simard, Rodney, Lavonne Mason, and Julie Abner. "I Defy Analysis: A Conversation with Gerald Vizenor." *Studies in American Indian Literatures* 5 (Fall 1993): 43–51.

Snyder, Michael. "From Orion to the Postindian: Vizenor's Movement Toward Postmodern Theory." *Across Cultures/Across Borders: Canadian Aboriginal and Native American Literatures*. Buffalo, N.Y.: Broadview Press, forthcoming.

Swann, Brian, and Arnold Krupat, eds. *I Tell You Now: Autobiographical Essays by Native American Writers*. Lincoln: University of Nebraska Press, 1987.

Velie, Alan. *Four American Indian Literary Masters*. Norman: University of Oklahoma Press, 1982.

———. "Gerald Vizenor's Indian Gothic." *MELUS* 17 (Spring 1991): 75–86.

———, ed. *Native American Perspectives on Literature and History*. Norman: University of Oklahoma Press, 1995.

Vizenor, Gerald, and A. Robert Lee. "Gerald Vizenor in Dialogue with A. Robert Lee." *Weber Studies* 16 (Winter 1999). http://weberstudies.weber.edu/archive/archive%20C%20Vol.%2016.2-18.1/Vol.%2016.2 /vizenorlee.html (accessed August 7, 2008).

Vizenor, Gerald, and A. Robert Lee. "Postindian Comments: Gerald Vizenor in Dialogue with A. Robert Lee." *Third Text* 43 (Summer 1998): 69–79.

Index